ANOTHER AMERICA

eds.

Scott Chamberlin
Donald Freed
Michael Gardner
Ara Mgrdichian

Acknowledgments
Pages 61-64: Excerpt from *Jesus Christs,* by A.J. Langguth, 1968,
2002, Figueroa Press. By permission of the author.
Page 171: "The Neurology in Shakespeare." Copyrighted 1989,
American Medical Association.
Cover: *Another America Meets the Corpulent Cowboy* (and book
design) by Scott Chamberlin, who extends due gratitude to
Peter Constable, Kiyo Marsh, and Eileen & Stephanie Barish.

Printed in the U.S.A.
ISBN 0-9745042-0-3

www.anotheramerica.org/anthology

For more information about this or future Another America titles, or
about attending Donald Freed's Saturday seminars in Los Angeles, please
e-mail theeditors@anotheramerica.org.

ANOTHER AMERICA

Contents

Foreword

America has made a lot of bad luck for itself—rather, its leaders have—but every time the Republic tottered, thinking Americans made some good luck:

The eighteenth century witnessed Tom Paine and Ben Franklin and the colonial printing press. The Lyceum and Chautauqua movements addressed the adult educational needs of the nineteenth century. The Book Clubs emerged after the culture-killing Great War of 1914-1918, and a flood of inexpensive paperbacks helped the nation recover from World War II.

Now is the hour of Print-on-Demand, just in time to meet and chart the drunken rhetoric of Shock and Awe.

The consolidated, embedded, behemoth American media were well primed for just this kind of war. "Good vs. Evil" is an ideal philosophical problem for giants.

With the nation's once-innumerable major publishers now consolidated to a mere six, the editors who remain in traditional publishing are shackled to the cold, numerical expectations of Wall Street. The corporations boost profits by promoting fewer authors and running larger print runs than ever before, leaving little room for contrary opinions, original storytelling, and new voices in general.

Yet today, with Print-on-Demand, making a book is almost as inexpensive per copy as printing thousands at a time. At little cost, an author or independent publisher can purchase an ISBN number, establish a title with a Print-on-Demand printer, and list a new book in the catalogues of booksellers. A buyer, whether ordering from a neighborhood bookstore or Amazon.com, need never know that the book had not been printed in advance by the tens of thousands.

Such is the case with the book in your hands, published by a collective of writers and readers to celebrate this emerging new freedom. Steve Wasserman, editor of the *Los Angeles Times Book Review,* recently cited the publishing legend Jason Epstein, describing a future in which a neighborhood bookstore need not build a costly, inherently risky, inventory of titles. An on-site

Print-on-Demand machine may take orders and create high-quality books with little more ceremony than it now takes to make an espresso. By this logic, even your neighborhood coffee shop could play that role, with your barista mercifully replacing the entire current distribution system.

As for the editors—they will be able to stop playing the gatekeeper, and return to their traditional role as the enabler and nurturer of America's literary tradition.

The future of publication will play out in venues yet to be imagined, but it is inherently linked to colorful advances in the historical record.

American literature had its beginning in the writings of Captain John Smith. As Smith tells his tale, he battled Turks in Hungary, was captured and escaped to Russia, battled Indians in the Powhatan Confederacy, was captured and famously escaped with the aid of Pocahontas to Plymouth, finally battled pirates in the Atlantic, and was captured and escaped penniless to England in 1616. In 1630 he published an account of his wanderings in *The True Travels and Adventures of Captaine John Smith in Europe, Asia, Africa, and America.*

It's instructive to read Smith's history with that of Cotton Mather's *Magnili Christi America*—a soldier of fortune alongside the fulminating rant from a New England pulpit. It is clear that the early Puritans were seeking freedom from English Anglicans. In the intervening centuries, the American soul has sought freedom from the Puritans.

Neither side of the equation is easily categorized. Each often stigmatizes the other. Smith was a noted cartographer and explorer. Mather matriculated to Harvard at age twelve. While in Boston he became a member of the Royal Society of London and corresponded with the noted chemist Robert Boyle. The preacher with his eye on Heaven while fearing the certain fall to Hell, and the soldiering mountebank with his foot planted firmly between the two is an American dichotomy that continues into the twenty-first century.

The seventeenth-century prose of Mather followed that of English ecclesiastics and Smith's followed the lead of English geographers. The eighteenth century produced writers who were finding their own voice. Benjamin Franklin's *Poor Richard's Almanac* was an American original, and the aphorisms of his unschooled Richard Saunters were a part of the American scene from 1732 through 1757. In 1727, he organized a symposium called the Leather Apron Club (or Junto Club), to debate subjects of political and scientific interest. This led to the establishment of the first public libraries in North America and the founding of the Academy of Philadelphia, later to become the University of Pennsylvania.

Early in the nineteenth century, the critical work and poetry of Edgar Allan Poe reached as far as Baudelaire's France. His tales and poetry told of a more darkly introspective American psyche and did little to alleviate the poverty and alcoholism to which the poet succumbed.

On a more populist note, Josiah Holbrook inaugurated the Lyceum movement in 1826. It spread from Millbury, Massachusetts, to 3,000 other locales within a half-dozen years. Holbrook rightly perceived that adult Americans were hungry for education. On the roster of the hundreds who taught and lectured were such luminaries as Henry David Thoreau, Nathaniel Hawthorne, and Ralph Waldo Emerson.

After the debacle of the American Civil War, the movement continued in New York's Lake Chautauqua under the auspices of William Rainey Harper. By 1900 the Chautauqua movement had formed its own publishing house and continued to thrive until the advent of World War I.

In *Democratic Vistas,* Walt Whitman suggested that:

> *The United States are destined to surmount the gorgeous history of feudalism or else prove the most tremendous failure of time.*

Mark Twain found American corruption and materialism throughout *The Gilded Age.* By the end of the century Herman Melville's *Moby Dick* had been forgotten and the author rated hardly a footnote in the American memory. Within a score of years, Henry Adams wondered if he and his fellow Americans were worth educating:

> *...most keen judges incline to think that barely one man in a hundred has a mind capable of reacting to any purpose on the forces that surround him, and fully half of these react wrongly.*

He later believed the American Dream of an educated class had faltered. Robinson Jeffers and William Faulkner elaborated: "America settles in the mold of its vulgarity, / heavily thickening to empire," wrote Jeffers. Faulkner had hoped that America would come to be "a sanctuary on the earth for the individual man." He later concluded that "…we dozed and slept, and the dream abandoned us."

Given the level of illiteracy in the United States, these are fair and fearful sentiments. One out of every five high school graduates faces a future with the reading skills of a fourth grader. Bilingual education has come close to zero education. Educational dysfunction is creating a new serfdom. Whitman's "gorgeous feudalism" is newly instated and it is anything but pretty.

The spirit of Franklin, Harper, and Holbrook might take cautious heart in the efforts collected hereafter. Another America asserts that a country of untapped intellectual resources has fallen beneath the media's narrow purview. Aside from the celebrated contributors contained within are numerous authors with whom the public is more-or-less unfamiliar.

Kevin "Bumdog" Torres has no forwarding address. In the parlance of our day he is a street person. Mr. William Wasz is numbered among the one percent of our population residing behind bars. He is a resident of the Mule Creek State Prison. Lance Fogan is a retired neurologist, amateur journalist, and professional grandfather. Adrienne Nater is a retired teacher, an aviator, and a surfboard champion. Mary Gilvarry is an Irish Catholic concerned with her church's redemption. Kristen Hren Moe is a mother and novelist. Barbara Ponse is a psychoanalyst, Frances Luban is a psychotherapist, and Patricia Rae Freed is a psychologist. Stephanie Silberstein and Lisa Haviland are graduate students at USC. Portia Putnam is an administrator with the Los Angeles Unified School District. Nina Hiken, Ara Mgrdichian, and Charles Kruger are teachers. Francine Kubrin is a hospital librarian. Tyler Craft Cormney is a business consultant and screenwriter. Richard Hellinga is a technical writer, and Susana Montal is a musician.

You'll find among them the young and the old, student and savant, rich and poor, the formally educated and the autodidactic, new writers finding their voice, and familiar masters at the height of their powers—whatever their status, each believes education to be a continuing affair. Fill in the blanks and you or your neighbors may be found within.

Included among Another America's friends are Harold Pinter, James Ragan, A.J. Langguth, Shelley Berman, Norman Corwin, Robert Altman, Ronald Harwood, Leon Katz, and colleagues at National Public Radio and the Department of Professional Writing at the University of Southern California.

From the above we have collected these pages. One of the more unusual moments is a collaboration between essay and aria. *"Otello:* An Introduction to a Prayer" concludes with Susana Montal's exquisite recital of Verdi's "Ave Maria." The two pieces were presented live at a Donald Freed Symposium; the former concludes this volume, and the latter can be downloaded at www.anotheramerica.org/avemaria.

Many of these authors will find their way in and through the Another America Press. This first effort will attract contributions for efforts still to come. These writers, those that follow, and the readers who find them will determine whether or not we become, as Whitman warned, "the most tremendous failure of time."

An America that can read is an America that can write and sing of open roads and of Ave Marias. Whitman believed, and so do we, that critical reading and writing—by the American people in their masses—is democracy.

The Comedian Jim MacGeorge
Shelley Berman

He comes to us aslant, like a man
uninvited, a good ear forward, lolling eyes
downward, a mouth at ease in a distantly
remembered smile. He stands to hear
his turn, drooping like a sunflower.

By the velour he walks his wait, turning
in the draping dark: to here, to there and back,
as if chasing down his whispers, as if prying
upon himself, or dancing to last night's laughter.
Now, abruptly he is still, and he braces to hear
his name.

He goes to the light, to the stage, as if without
intention, as if wary of the floor, as if weighing
a knock on a door so as to sell a brush
bravely while hoping there is no answer.
Yet, with wise eyes beading, he is opening
his case.

Lines crack like Astaire's torpedoes, cannonades
of sudden laughter; the stage is a jubilant
realm as he peoples his court with kings' voices,
with each jut of the jaw or the lip, new face after
face familiar. Now, shuffling with foxy grace,
he smiles to his applause.

He comes off as a man home from work, seeking
a place for his cap; his still lolling eyes held wide,
surprised by the grip of new darkness. In the quiet
he loosens his waist, perhaps ponders
a moment that failed, then, recalling his
laughter he stands, drooping like a sunflower.

Mr. L
Francine Kubrin

An old man stands in his front doorway, squinting at the bright summer light. He wears scuffed loafers, sweat pants, and a long-sleeved business shirt tucked into the draw-string waist band. A middle-aged Asian woman in a white uniform stands at his side. "Take my arm, Mr. L," she says firmly as he steps over the threshold. "Get away from me," he yells. She frowns, steps back a few paces and follows him as he limps across the lawn, rubbing his hip.

Mr. L walks towards two young Hispanic men waiting at the curb. One of the men wears a tank top, baggy pants and is tying a red bandana around his head, a tattooed dragon covers his left bicep. The other man, in cut-off jeans and a t-shirt with the name of a rock group, wears earphones and bobs his head to the silent beat of the music.

Mr. L looks at the two younger men: "Ugh, ugh, hi there. I'm Mr. L. You, you, you'll be moving everything from my house and garage into those things," pointing to two curbside storage containers. "Before you start, there's a couple of things I want to tell you. Don't, don't leave anything behind, including the stuff in the garage. Do you hear me clearly?" The man with the earphones says, "Relax, señor, we do this all the time, don't worry." "You, you, you be sure you don't forget any thing, and I mean anything, or you'll be sorry you ever met me."

He turns his back on the men and shuffles over to the pair of storage containers: walks around them, taps the exterior wood slabs and peers fearfully into the empty darkness as if the orifices were the gaping jaws of hungry beasts. He covers his mouth and clears his throat, like a man stifling a cry.

Mr. L watches the men fill the containers with household furnishings. He strokes the arm of an overstuffed chair as the men wrestle it into a container. "Move, señor, or you'll get hurt," shouts the man with the earphones.

Mr. L whispers the name of each piece of furniture. He grabs the man with the bandana by the arm. "Listen, listen, you've got the boxes of photographs. I, I don't want anything to happen to those old pictures so be very careful with them.

Stack them away from the other things." The man shoves the box into a corner of the container.

Mr. L scowls and looks towards the street, a rivulet of heat rises from the asphalt, sweat rolls down his seamed face. He removes a monogrammed handkerchief from his shirt pocket and wipes his face and neck. The sound of a barking dog pierces the hot stillness. A car drives by, its windows sealed against the heat. A pedestrian hurries by and glances at the moving men. Mr. L stands by the containers like a sentry.

The woman watches Mr. L wiping his brow. "I'll be right back," she says, heading into the house, and emerges a few minutes later carrying four bottles of water and a folding chair. She taps Mr. L on the shoulder, pointing to the chair, "We're not packing this thing, are we?" He eases himself onto the chair. "No, we're not." Her hand is on the back of the chair. Mr. L sips the bottled water. "This stuff is lousy. I want a cold beer." "Now, Mr. L, you know you can't have beer. Drink some more water." She turned away from the old man and handed each of the Latinos a bottle of water.

"We're almost done moving everything out," says the man with the earphones. "These boxes of rocks?" "I use the rocks for hydroponics gardening," says Mr. L. "Have you ever heard of that? Of course, you haven't. You don't know a damn thing. Believe me, I could tell you a thing or two but you wouldn't listen." The young man's jaw tightens, he looks down and thrusts his hands into his pockets. As he trudges back to the garage, he pulls one hand out of his pocket and cuffs his fingers. He massages his jaw with his knuckles, casting a sidelong glance at Mr. L.

"We're leaving now," the man with the bandana announces. "Wait a minute, you can't leave yet," shouts Mr. L, scuffling towards the house, followed by the woman. A few minutes later, the pair emerge from the darkened house. The old man slouches, clutching a packet of unopened mail. "Okay, okay, now you can go. Get the hell out of here!" He closes the front door, listening to its hollow sound.

He watches the men shut the double doors, winces at the resounding snap of the crowbars fastening each container. He turns towards the men as they roll them over a ramp and into a van. The man in the bandana climbs into the cab, removes his head cover and starts the engine. The other man snaps on his earphones, sways to the music. "Here, señor," he plops the set of padlock keys into Mr. L's open palm. The old man stares at the keys and drops them into his shirt pocket.

He watches the van drive off until it fades from view. He blinks and wipes his eyes. His shoulders slump, he stumbles towards a car. The woman links her arm in his and guides him to the passenger seat. He sighs, leans back against the headrest, and covers his eyes with his hand.

As the car turns the corner onto a tree-lined street, he looks out between his fingers at the shadows. "We're almost there, Mr L."

"I know, I know," he whispers.

Orange Diamonds
A Novel in Progress
Kristine Hren Moe

Chapter 1
The Wedding Reception—June 21, 1997, 8:25 p.m.

Up and down. Side to side. Side to side. In and out. Skip here. Skip there. In and *ahh—my foot!* I slid back, my cheek plastered to Joe's drenched white shirt. He said, "I always said you should have married me."

The DJ bounced from side to side; Joe bounced along with him—my body caught somewhere in between like a basketball dribbled too hard. I pushed him away and peeled the yellow power tie left over from the '80s off my face. My sister's arm brushed me as she and her husband spun past like a two-in-one spinning top, their feet taunting one another but never touching. She raised an eye and gave me the look that meant *better you than me.* Joe smiled.

"You ready?" Joe's left arm already pushing, his right hand high on my back, pinning my chest to his belly so that I would not float away from him like the woman in Chagall's *Promenade.* Joe—my family's lifelong neighbor who still lived with his eighty-year-old mother. Joe—It seemed wrong to be conjuring Chagall against his fat belly, and him knowing nothing about it. "Great deejay," Joe took a breath and spun me around. The polka bounced from wall to wall and rushed out through the open glass doors. I closed my eyes, breathed in jolts of the warm evening air, and tried to get the painting out of my head.

Father Bogomir had smiled across the altar during the ceremony earlier that day. "The perfect omen for bride and groom," his head haloed by rays of sunlight filtered through the stained glass window of the Virgin Mary, "Sun is always good, but rain on a wedding day portends vast wealth and happiness to come. You and Graham will be King and Queen of Persia. Of *India Karamandia.*" A baby's squeal burst into the vaulted ceiling, then ricocheted from painted stucco wall to wall to marble floor, followed by the click of heels. I squeezed Graham's hand; he winked at me and dabbed the side of his face with a handkerchief.

Now Joe's arm pasted onto mine. I lifted my arm and let it hover in the air. Back and forth, side to side. "One, two, three. One, two, three," Joe whispered. I imagined Graham's arm wrapped around my waist, leading me around the dance floor, our feet moving in unison, spinning as if we two belonged to one great orb— *"So we grew together / Like to a double cherry seeming parted—Hermia, or was it Helena? A Midnight Summer's—I'm all mixed up—Stop the quotes!*

A drop of sweat fell onto my hand and I opened my eyes. "It's a sauna in here," Joe said. Couples maneuvered their way around us, heels grazing my toes. My best friend Lydi bit her lip and made a face as she circled past. Her husband was a homegrown Slovene, imported just for her. He worked in my uncle's machine shop, once in a while, but he sure could dance.

Joe pulled out a tissue and wiped his face and blew his nose in one swoop. "Let's get a drink," I said. My sister Anna eyed me from across the dance floor. "You ain't getting out of this so fast. You'd think they'd put on some air-conditioning," he pushed the wet ringlets of hair from his eyes.

"Why don't we try it like this then," I grabbed Joe's hand. "Ah, there's a piece of tissue stuck right—" Joe wiped his forehead, and I tried to move him from side to side. Joe laughed at me. "You aren't supposed to lead." He pulled me to his chest, swung me around, and began hopping again. The polka could not last forever. I gave in. His belly made a wavelike motion. "One, two, three. One, two, three." He counted the polka's rhythm under his breath, then took the leap of faith and spoke again.

"It should have been me and you tonight." I caught myself nodding my head, and stopped, pretending I hadn't heard a word. "You truly are the most beautiful woman I've ever seen." Joe turned me to the right. "I waited too long." I held my breath, and watched the lights strike the disco ball and shimmer off the top of circling heads, then away through the glass doors and out to the darkening sky. Graham sat just outside the door surrounded by old college friends. The patio tables were uncovered, their cloths soaked by the afternoon rain.

"You're stiff as a board," Joe said. "Sor—" I stopped my-

self. He followed my eye and looked over his shoulder. "Oh."
That's all he said, then squeezed me tighter, turned me faster,
"One, two, three. One, two, three." His whisper turned into a
wheeze. The smell of cheap musk and Irish Spring enveloped
me. I held my breath. The scent of Joe would never leave me,
the heat and moisture of his body searing the spoor into my
dress, my skin—*"Through every hollow cave and alley lone / Round
and round the spicy downs the yellow Lotus dust is blown."*

"Huh?" Joe said. I stopped. I had breathed the words out
loud. "Tennyson—Nothing," I bit my lower lip and counted
how long I could hold my breath and twirled to the left, to the
right.

"Michael—no!" My mother-in-law Rosalind unraveled in
front of me. She clutched the fuchsia ties that held her criss-
crossed top together, so that her floral bra poked through as
her ex-husband Michael held her by the nook of his arm, then
brought her back to his chest. Rosalind reached her hand out to
me like a child suddenly realizing that her feet did not reach the
bottom of the pool. "I told Michael this isn't a country western.
He keeps twirling me around like I'm some twenty-year-old."
Michael laughed and pulled her back to him. The dress hugged
Rosalind as the two spun away, their steps synchronized as if
ten years had never found them apart. Her hair was a polished
red, each strand glazed into a line that led to her cheekbone.
Rosalind looked over her shoulder, "Are you all right, dear?"
She was gone before I could answer.

"They sure are a good-looking couple," Joe said. The room
spun; I pressed forward and clenched my fists. *The song had lasted long enough.* I put my right foot forward and smashed his toes.
He looked around the dance floor in horror as he stumbled
backward. I reached out my hand, "Joe!" He staggered back,
bumped into Magda, my mother's best friend, who frowned as
she looked him up and down, "Didn't you mami teach you how
to dance?" "My mom's an American," Joe said. Magda grunted
and her son Johnnie moved her across the floor.

Joe looked at me, waiting for some sort of—*One dance. That
was all that was expected.* Well, one complete one. Joe pushed his
tongue against the roof of his mouth. "I think I've had enough,"
he cleared his throat, pulled up his pants, and tucked in the edge
of his shirt. "D'you mind if we get a drink." He shifted his leg
and looked at the floor. "My foot's kinda sore."

"Oh, okay, if you want," I said, "you go ahead," and headed for the door, trying not to notice Joe limping toward the bar. My cousin Stanley winked at me and my blue-haired Aunt Vesna watched me from the table next to the dance floor. She puckered her lips together, leaned forward, and extended her hand. "That Joe's a nice boy." My aunt grabbed a hold of my arm. "But he's too old." She smiled, her dentures glowing under the rainbow of lights, and patted me on the behind. I smiled and lowered my eyes as I escaped, skirting along the edge of the dance floor, heading for the glass door.

The polka ended as I worked my way toward Graham, and a waltz began. Coupled men and women whirled left and right, counterclockwise around the floor. Two young girls ran past squealing; a boy jumped over a chair and knocked it down. I sidestepped him and backed into the industrial beige curtains that had been tied to the wall with white ribbon. The photographer raised his flash above my head and I gave the canned smile that cameras interpret as a grimace. Antlers jutted from above. I pushed the curtain back, and the black marbled eyes of a stuffed, moth-eaten elk stared down at me. The last mount still hanging on the trophy wall, waiting for the janitor to throw it in the trash before the next girl smeared lipstick on its lips, before another boy stuck a cigarette in its mouth.

"That was quite a shot," the photographer laughed. "A stuffed elk and you."

I pushed past the photographer, past a table of Slovenes who had greeted my parents into the States in the mid-sixties: "Beautiful dress." "Such a beautiful girl." "I remember when you were so young." "Dis place is really nice." "The stone walls—nice touch—I never been here." I had added them to the guest list out of respect for my parents. A woman leaned close to her husband's ear. "How did Peter afford dis school?" I wasn't supposed to hear that. I stopped and turned around. The woman paused, then smiled. My father had helped her husband stand guard at his meat market in 1966 when the riots threatened the neighborhood. The woman pulled me down to her buxom chest. "You Mami and Ati so proud." Her kiss slid across my cheek and landed on my arm.

"So nice of you to come," I said.

"I vouldn't miss it for d' vorld." She pushed me away. "You should be dancing." I moved closer to the empty tables lining the wall. Plates of half-eaten cake and drinks not yet finished were scattered across the white linen.

"Kati." My sister's hand was already wrapped around my arm. "Quite a move out there." Anna turned me around and licked her thumb. "That woman got lipstick all over you."

"There should be a warning label," I said. "It's Joe," Anna said. "You lasted longer than I would have." She pressed her thumb into my cheek and wiped away. "I think he gave me a blister, look." I tried to bend over to show, but Anna held onto my chin. "Would you please stop!" I said.

"I can't believe it."

"What?"

"Look at this!" All I saw were the blonde highlights bursting from Anna's brown hair. "How can I see anything with your head in my way?" Anna tugged at my bodice and stepped away for a bird's-eye view. Anna's husband Boris edged to her side. "Honey, it's really not that bad." He was always right behind her. "Not that bad?" Anna raised her voice, making sure that everyone who had not seen the fuchsia trail across my bodice would see it now. "Boris, get my purse." Boris darted through the tables, past the old Slovenes. Anna brought the edges of silk together and rubbed, sounding like our mother years ago bent over the basement sink, washing our socks. *If you can't wear slippers in the house, then you can wash your own socks!* Then she would look at my bare feet: *Kje so sopate?* I won't watch you standing barefoot on the cement floor! My mother would say this and rub the dirt of one sock into the other—somehow they always came out clean.

I looked down at my chest. The fuchsia trail had turned to mauve. "You're just smearing it in," I fought Anna's hands away—her lips twisted and her eyes dropped. "I was only trying to help." "Well—" "Well?" "Just use some water," I grabbed a linen napkin and dunked it into the pitcher of water on the table beside us. "Here." I stuffed the cloth into Anna's hand and she wrapped it around her finger, circled the water deep into the fiber of my dress, prodding the stain out of the fabric. Finally Anna spoke. "Did you smell that woman's perfume?" Anna giggled and for an instant she was my pimple-faced sister bellowing "Ave Maria" as she strummed the chords of her electric guitar on top of her bed, her walls pasted with images of Sean Cassidy. I leaned onto her shoulder, pulled the strap of my sandal over the blister, and winced.

"Hey, Fred and Ginger!" The photographer snapped a picture of my mother and Rosalind's boyfriend Harold as they rocked from side to side—my mother's eyebrow raised like Anna's over her salmon-colored glasses, questioning the whole motion. Her dark brown hair had been dyed especially for the wedding, teased and sprayed one time too many. Harold twirled her around, brought her closer, put on his best smile, and the photographer walked away.

Anna turned to the dance floor, "Mom really should have bought a size bigger." My mother wore a silk mauve dress with a lace overlay "to hide her stomach," but it had bunched over it instead. Anna slid her hands over the shiny coral taffeta of her bridesmaid dress, "I guess I shouldn't talk." I had said they could choose whatever dresses they wanted—*but taffeta?* She pursed her lips, "You're not far behind, you know."

"I didn't say anything." I looked back at the dance floor. "Just wait until you have kids," Anna said. Harold turned his head from side to side, his eye always on Rosalind. "It's not about you then," Anna said. "Do you have any gum?" "Where would I put it?" She frowned, "I think I have some in my purse," then she looked from the stain to my mother.

My mother grinned, let her eyes fall to the floor, her back turned ever so slightly. It was as if with each passing year she was slowly turning into the very image of my grandmother, her body bending over the earth, her long white hair braided and pinned under the babushka, as she raked hay down rolling hills in a row of singing women. I had only seen pictures, heard stories. Sort of like *The Gleaners, Jean Francois Millet,* but—no—too French. Anna brought the wet napkin to my dress and began to rub again. "I just hope this comes out." *En hribcek bom kupil, bom trte sadil,* the words ran in a circle through my mind. Every summer my father driving the wood-paneled Volaré station wagon, and Anna and I belting out the songs with our mother as we headed for the Atlantic Ocean for summer vacation. My mother would act as beach patrol calling us in from the waters she could not swim: "Sharks!" I would swim further until I could barely see her hand waving me back in. "Katya, come back, too far!" My mother preferred the mountains: "I'll buy a little hill, and there I'll plant vines"—the English translation never as beautiful. Anna looked at me; I watched my mother.

My mother would look at me look at her trying on a new dress or pair of pants in a department store. *Ne gledat v moj speh.* "Don't look at my fat," she would say with a laugh and quickly turn to cover the rolls. I would just shake my head. It was a rare occasion that she would actually try on clothes before me, always insisting that she had plenty of clothes for work. *Gledemo za tebe, ne za mene.* "We're looking for you, not for me. You need clothes for school." And so we would rush past her department toward mine—dinner had to be on the stove by four-thirty to be ready by the time my father came home from work at a quarter 'til six.

"She doesn't need a new dress every time." "She's a growing girl, Ati." My father and mother would argue back and forth when the next Slovenian event was approaching—usually a wedding of someone I hardly knew or the performance of the singing groups *Korotan* or *Fantje na Vasi,* "Boys in the Village" though they were hardly boys anymore—my mother's hand already wrapped around the car keys. "Go, just go," my father would say, waving us from his side. My mother and I running out the door. "Let's go to Saks," she squeezing my leg, grinning from ear to ear: "We have just enough time." And so we would enter, our rubber heels squeaking past the high-heeled clicks on the polished white floors, two trespassers headed for the "Evening" section, always aware of the salesperson watching us; inspecting the seams closely, closely, feeling the nubs of silk between our fingers, turning the sales ticket over when the person wasn't looking—the devious smile: we knew we could copy the masterpiece for an eighth of the price.

Another polka started. I twisted a bead of my gathered skirt between my fingers and watched them dance. Saks had been for special occasions: "They have quality"; Sears for every day. I twisted the bead. My mother had sewn the beads on my wedding dress one by one.

Anna looked back up at me. "You can hardly see it, Katya."

Song
Patricia Rae Freed

What luck!
Got it for free
Never had to go out and find
That father of mine:
"Say," whatever your name is,
"I'm the little girl you walked out on.
Some thirty years it's been now."
No.
He just swung right into
That hospital room
Visiting, we were,
A mutual and ailing relation.
Held on to my chair, I did
And said:
"Steady now."

The shock of his aging
Hit me first.
It didn't help that
Jowls
Hung
Under
Three days stubble.
Eyes, badly focused
Crusted with clear, thin, ice.
Tobacco had done its job
On those two front teeth
Or was their color due
To simple decay?
There was
Fat

Bulging
Beneath a cowboy shirt
But the tweed jacket
And the plaid fedora
Had the look of a man
Who knows a good cut
When he sees one
That jaunty hat
Shielding so well
A vanity about baldness
I remembered from
Another life.

"Well," he said
Timorous
The eyes had always rimmed red so easily
"It's all come to me too late."
Knowing now I had the upper hand
I rallied:
"Think of those it never comes to at all."
Added, still enjoying the sport:
"Is it clean money at least?"
Money is money!
Only against the law if you get caught!
A sickness if you lose!
Be a winner and you'll live forever!
This, his answer,
Refrains again,
From my past.

"Oh! I have a friend," I offer,
"He deals in dope
Pimping,

Perhaps you know each other..."
Reverting to another pattern
Moralizing to my no good old man
He shakes his head
As if to say:
"I never could win with you."
With my Mother either
I wanted to yell
But finally did say
Out loud
How hard it must have been
To fight her perfection
How hard to be rescued
From her strength.

So
From this
I got him to talk
About his five wives
Always with the jokes
He tells me next time
He'll have to be listed
In the yellow pages.
Not under "fathers"
Someone says in my head
But I want
More than anything
For him to be proud of me
So I say nothing
Then I go about
Verifying some facts:
"You did give me a set of golf clubs

When I was born?"
Not saying:
"That meant you loved me
Or at least had some hopes."

There we stood
Like two lovers
Trying to talk
Over the din
Of a dying woman
Whose hand I'd forgotten
I was clutching.
Could it be on this
Her death bed,
That she recovered herself
In the presence of father and child
Enough to see
Enough to hear
My slightest murmur of a reply when he
Finally asked:
"Could we have lunch sometime?
Not even God would have to know."
"It's a possibility,
I'll think it over."
"Anything is a possibility in this life…"
Says my hardened old aunt
And she relaxes at last
Back to the pillows
Against which she's been straining
To hear
This song.

A Quiet Life
A Novel in Progress
Frances Luban

Anne found remnants of her aunt's life in the closets of her empty apartment in an East Bay suburb a few days after she died. A black silk evening cloak in the style of the forties, a dozen high-school graduation photographs in their cardboard frames, a plush toy that was a replica of the Velveteen Rabbit. An eighty-year-old woman who had never married, had her aunt left these objects as clues for Anne to the mystery of her life? As Anne picked up cards and letters scattered on the floor, she saw that a dozen had been opened by her aunt before she went to the hospital. She read the messages: "All my love, Martin"; "Haven't seen you all day, miss you. Love, Martin"; "Until tonight—with much love, Martin."

The absence of her aunt was a presence in the room. Anne walked around, looking at familiar objects in the twilight as if she had never seen them before. Now it was too late to ask the questions that flooded her mind about her aunt, about her family, about herself. There was no one to tell, no one to ask.

She shivered. A sharp December wind with the promise of a storm shook the trees outside the sliding glass doors of the balcony. She turned on the lights, then turned them off. Dusk seemed the only atmosphere to contain the ghosts that swirled around the room. Her understanding of her aunt's life, her own life, dissolved into the shadows. The certainties she had structured into a complicated existence were disappearing.

She paced the room, pausing before the framed photographs on the two Victorian lamp tables. There were snapshots of Anne with her husband, with her daughter, with her granddaughter, who wore a clown costume and rouged cheeks in celebration of Purim. Anne leaned closer and looked into the pictures, searching for herself.

Anne had come to inventory and empty the apartment. The manager of the building had made it clear that the rent was paid for only three more days as he gave her the keys. Dazed by her discovery of her aunt's hidden life, she forgot her task. Her instinct was to flee back to her orderly life, where things were what they seemed, to go back to her hotel, to call her husband, to say—what?

She stood still in the darkening room, then as if on command, she walked to her aunt's closet. In the half-light, Anne opened the door and took the black silk coat from its hanger and put it on over her wool sweater and skirt. A faint fragrance surrounded her. It was a perfume, "Jicky," by Guerlain, that Anne had long ago chosen for her own.

Anne looked at herself in the long pier glass in her aunt's bedroom. There was just enough light filtering through the east window. The coat fit her perfectly.

Covers of Comfort
Adrienne Nater

Little girl, a joy to behold, Bright
Blue eyes, beneath the tented bed covers
The flashlight flickers in the dark room
Book open, pictures glitter, words live.
The handsome horse, dapple-gray, red hooves
Lives in this book; he whispers,

"Little girl, all alone, join a friend
Ride the carousel
Into the world of lights and shadows
Circular travels, the tethered body
The unfettered soul."

Beautiful horse, noble creature, wondrous friend
Speaking the coded language.
Black on white, squiggles and lines
Familiar sounds, loving messages.
Safely hidden from outside worlds.

Blond, graceful hands, dancer's legs
Moving noiselessly toward the closed door: Mother
Hush, little girl, fear naught
Become immersed; be reassured

Life is a circular thing.

Every Third House
A Novel in Progress
Donald Freed

Editors' Note:
Below is a letter from prison, written in 1974: Part of a correspon-
dence between a Black Panther leader and his unindicted co-conspira-
tor, a white, wealthy poet.

I have my multi dictionary here (thanks) and it tells me that
the original Greek *Agon* or "trial of strength" is the common
ancestor of our "trial" system of law along with the "sport"
of wrestling, boxing etc. where the antagonists struggled for
victory (because "Victory" is the aim, of the struggle or the
trial, and *not* "*Justice.*") In any political trial the State must claim
victory and it always does except where the "fix is equal." The
Power of the State is irresistible except for the power of the
people. The way you "fix" the legal process is by introducing
popular power ("judicious indignation") into the courtroom,
the jury room, the media, etc. This process is vulgar as hell and
to get your hands on the dynamics of what happened in all those
political trials we won and the few, like mine, that we lost you
need to have gone to Mike Mule's Arena on Wednesday nights
with Addie Mae Gatewood.

You start off walking right after supper, first dark, up Lee
Street through what we used to call the "Quarter." Poor as it
was, dingy and shadowy and cheap as it was, Lee Street was full
of life. Full of life. Walk on past the shine stands and the barber
shops and the beauty parlors and notions shops (can anybody
tell me why the American Black is *the* cleanest and most com-
pulsively groomed and shined and shaved pauper in the world?
And especially in the South where Addie made sixty dollars a
month in those days of the late '40's).

Through the rough R & B from the juke joints bouncing
off the street, Granny greeting old acquaintances as she stalked

along with me trotting behind until we reached the snow cone stand and stopped to buy a paper dish filled with strawberry colored crushed ice. Sweet and cold. Then we were there, Mike Mule's Arena! Lord have mercy.

Mike Mule's Arena was a sprawling ramshackle old firetrap, covered in front with thirty years of wrestling posters, with separate entrances for Colored and White (like every other facility of that time), and Mike Mule, himself, stood right in front on the sidewalk in his suspenders and panama hat with a stump of a stogie clamped in his iron jaws, heavyset in his 60's (that was old then) nodding his head in a set smile (I looked up to him then, now I see he could have been Adolf Eichmann standing smiling the way they did, at the entrance to a concentration camp, smiling and nodding and barking out "Right – Left – Right.")

Anyway, we'd go into the hollow echo and peanut smell and sweat of the hall and climb up to the Nigger Section. The excitement. Old and young were as high as for a Super Bowl today, and down below the white people, too, just as high, and most all of them working class or lower. Then the old fire bell rang and Ben Levy (a fireman, himself) shuffled into the ring and the light in the hall went down and the limelight covered the ring and five hundred true believers leaned forward in an act of faith.

"Ladies and Gentlemen, the first match of the evening, with a 30 minute time-limit, from Norman, Oklahoma, weighing 203 pounds—Chief Little Beaver! From Brooklyn, New York, weighing 211 pounds, Angelo Cistoli!"

Before we get carried away here trying to be Ernest Hemingway, let me make the point about the fix being equal in the courtroom and how that fix allowed for some alternative to violence. Alright—you know that all the matches at Mike Mule's were fixed, as they are everywhere up to this minute, and everyone in the audience knew then, as they do now, that the matches were fixed, that those big burly men wrestled in a different town every night of the week and then after all the grunting and groaning they would be seen at the best Bar and Grill in town eating big steaks together. But here is the point: we knew but we suspended our disbelief exactly as you would watching *Hamlet*, we knew and we didn't know; to the wrestling audience this is not a Sport it is Theater, it is Drama and secretly it is life and death politics.

When Leroy "Jack" McGurk (who had been a college champion and was not fat and could actually wrestle in the Greek style, and could have been a great champion if it had been a sport), when he triumphed over that greaseball of evil incarnate, Juan Humberto (from Mexico City, Mexico, at a sleek 220 pounds of rippling muscle and grease with slick black hair and a scarred face, looking like Anthony Quinn), we were in heaven because the clean white hard-muscled gladiator Jack McGurk had vanquished the dark and dirty Mexican.

Jack McGurk the All-American Boy was our white hope, our champion in the morality play of good and evil. These things have to be fixed so that Good can win, *every time.* There is no place for chance in art or a lumpenproletariat art form like modern American wrestling, because there has to always be a place, one place, (now on T. V.) where there is *justice;* where the man who has been savaging the hero (biting and gouging and strangling and cutting and garlic and tape and, once, the Green Mask pulled out a bottle of knockout drops and Addie Mae had to be held back), destroying our hero—while the blind Ben Levy, the referee, saw nothing and never heard our howls of pity and outrage—where this monster would at the last moment of moral and physical anguish be, himself, overthrown and quickly counted out.

The Educated Class—Left or Right—watches this spectacle in the arena, shakes its head and pronounces the fixed and obviously faked events as the extreme of mass False Consciousness in America. But I can show you why that judgment misses the point. The Proletariat and the lumpenproletariat want something that is a combination of Justice and Revenge. They want an election, they want a trial, they want a wrestling match, and in a Democracy the underdog must always win; the hero is not a Caesarean lion devouring a helpless Christian, the hero is an abused and battered victim of villainous dirty tricks who pulls himself up off the mat, and with the transported and invincible crowd climbing out of their seats with their eyes and mouths torn open in one unbroken and terrific roar of anguish and triumph our ruined champion brushes aside the suddenly vigilant referee and confronts Evil! Evil begging, pleading for mercy from the Avenger, from us, the crowd, but no, this is not a Greek tragedy, there's no pity here because this is an American tragedy, and when the moment of truth comes there can be no pity, no thought of pity, but our champion, just to be sure, turns to the audience open handed, while Evil grovels, and we (We, not Caesar), we cry out Evil's doom, and Good turns on the sub-human monster at his feet and drags the thing up on its legs and Good smashes Evil to the canvas (pretends to, no man could live through such a beating one night much less *every* night) over and over and over again, then Falls on him for the count. The bell clangs, the winner's arm is raised, the hall lights come back on, the big wrestlers in their shiny silk robes wave and chat as they walk back to their dank dressing rooms—and we, we the judge and jury, the life blood of the winner, we are spent, exhausted, revenged, and saved. We can go home now.

You say that the Ruling Class uses precisely such "two party" spectacles and rituals as a counter-revolutionary hypnosis so as to keep the Masses in a permanent and passive trance. That is only partly true and must, also, be placed in context. The problem is that the we who watch and weep in this arena, we know, too, that it is a fake! Yes! The masses know it as well as the Ruling Class, and what's more, in the same repressed way we know that Mike Mule's Arena is a house of illusion, we also know that the White House and the Supreme Court and the Pentagon are too! You don't know that but we do. But we know that only in *our* house of dreams is the violence *faked*. Because there the fix is in for us. But in all the official arenas of the State the violence is real and we are the unrisen underdog and canon fodder without end. But the Educated Class can't see the absolute hoax of the State, the Academy, the Party, the Church, etc. as they can so exactly see through the wrestling ritual. Only the Ruling Class and the Masses know that it's all fake, from top to bottom. But the retribution and violence for challenging this official hoax is real and terrible—so the Masses strike a silent bargain with the State: the two extremes on the social scale conspire not to reveal to the middle and educated classes the absolute lies on which their happy lives are all based.

You know only too well what happens when the zombie wakes up. In our arrest and trial it was not black man and white woman sex that brought on the legal circus, not even the spectacle of Kissinger and Rockefeller at "risk," and not just your money and name alone. It was the *combination* of the Ivy League Debutante and the Nigger, in bed together *politically!* That was too much. Too much for the State and too much for the jurors, White and Black, whose counterparts had been pardoning Black Panthers who *had* broken the "Law" across the country. If we had been in the courtroom chained together we would have won, no question about it, but with you an "unindicted co-conspirator" and media victim, we never had a chance. You understand, don't you, that if we *had* been guilty, *had* kidnapped Kissinger, and *had* been tried together in chains then we *would* have had a real chance, an overwhelming probability of a hung jury (not that they would ever have let us go)!

Shall I take pity on the poor pig who has to read all this and wind it up? We who sit in the Nigger Section and the prisoner's dock—not in the jury box—we know all about the invisible violence behind the black robes and the flag and the documents and all the emblems of State and Church, and out of this fear that dogs us night and day we invent a new identity that can survive with what we hope is a shred of dignity to cover our naked terror and so we hide out in Mike Mule's Arena A.K.A. City Hall and cover our ass with the flag. So the fake violence inside the Arena is a cover for the down-on-one-knee plea for mercy that we, the villain, beg for; & this spectacle inside the arena in conjunction with the scenario outside—Law and Order—completely mistakes the relationship of forces between the "individual" and the State and scrambles the brains of the spectators (did I ever tell you about how the police when they used to stop us to frisk us up against a police car they would jab you with a pin so that you'd jump and swing out and then the pigs would close in and beat you silly, but remember in the wrestling matches the Bad Guy always rubbed tape or garlic in the Good Guy's eyes until blinded and mad with pain the sleeping giant of virtue awoke to his full powers and showed *the villain* no mercy, so if you turn the arena and the street on their head then the two spectacles for Good and Evil and Law and Order equal each other and everybody lives and dies in one long riff of false consciousness in which the idea of Violence and Non-violence are control codes to keep the band playing until the party's over).

Where does all this leave the Black Panther Party? Nowhere because we haven't even *begun* that discussion, we've just been talking about the *context* for the discussion, the Idea not the Act much less the Idea of the Act, and I don't believe I could go too much further without boiling all these metaphors down to a scientific historical base & I question whether I have any of the requirements (except the time!) to do that. Maybe you could boil it all *up*—because you're the poet.

I think of you. You know what that means. You're the poet.

All Power to the People,

L.

***

Windshield
Ara Mgrdichian

Scenic routes and rumbling trees
a transient sight, an ephemeral green
something rustles underneath
across the bank of gray
a tinge of red
and mammalian breath
riding the hard concrete

a smudge on glass?
an irritant?

brazen and dislodged
the blood and guts of smaller things
broken against your eye

inert now
[like you now]

blind and mute and deaf and dumb

*

give us a smudge, an anomaly
along with waves of grain
purple mounds and majesty
defying rooted lanes
give us respite from news and Love
and give us our daily bread

give us more dead bugs against the glass
a cow on a hill ... a water tank
and the long liquescent road

Hemispheres
James Ragan

Fathers of the East

I

It is when your eyelids fell across the Atlantic,
in pooled darkness, or when the spider of your lash
fluttered to lave the wheat in Danube earth,
or when you danced the high snows of the Tatras
to see the new moon tossed
in ruins among the winter birch.
It is when you slept on the Ellis Island deck
in the fantasy of being what is and what's not,
little more than a comma
in the eternal sentence of a nation's thought,
drifting, in and out, a raft to a torn rock,
as if by mourning all the fathers war had lost,
you could build your house, America,
with mud, and blood and splintered talk,
and tame the mule of your foreign tongue
with stubborn words that poems exact.
I have wanted to be like that.

II

It is when your infant sons had cradled far
from the mother's breast, the long leaf of pride
unbudding from their muscled tongues,
and bodies, lean as warring gods,
unhoused the winter in their hearts,
or when your daughters warmed
in moonlight at the window's shutter,
waiting for the sun to root
through eyes of keys and locks,
through all the doors the world had chained,
the mansions built, the rooms uncrossed
to where the promised ball of order
had dried to mouldered dust.
It is when all gods would sound the same,
you found their laugh in all things lost.

Sons of the West

I

We have seen the sun blister on Manhattan,
heard the rivering lip of the Asian sun
rend its consonants and vowels
into the rime of a tyrant's argument.
Long before we crossed the desert's whistling rill
to where the faith in frenzy breeds half-crazed gods,
long before we tented all beliefs
in the incubating bed of lesser thought,
we gave the pessimist our hand, and shook it
for what little knowledge truth could stand.

II

I, too, in the death-wick of the Kennedy days
drifted blindly through the innocent loss.
I, too, trembling, through the fires of a Tien An Men lamp,
wept my pillows into mirrors of glass,
and with my thoughts
fractured daily by its abstract glance,
I have come to know so little of something
or nothing at all. And out of compassion
have I taken the path to forgiven history
to know what hemispheres of the heart
I've yet to cross. What cicatrix of a world-wound
a single word might heal, remembering
how frayed the ill-knit bond
between my vision and my will,
remembering how high into your mind I'd gone,
 and on whose broad shoulder I had climbed
  to wail my words to the ancients and the world beyond.

The Cornfields
A Novel in Progress
Scott Chamberlin

2

Sidney's door was ajar, so Paul let himself inside and stood quietly in the narrow white entryway.

Listening, he found an empty wall and leaned in silence, facing a metal rack he had never noticed before.

Sidney had used the rack in perfect compliance with its manufacturer's expectations, storing a fedora and a baseball cap ("Mets") on the top rack, a half-dozen coats that hung down to various lengths, and pairs of shoes lined up beneath. A picturesque woven scarf had been tied to the rack and hung alongside the coats. Between this fixture and the door, slightly off center, a single hook dangled an undecorated ring with three keys.

Paul stuffed his hands into his jacket pockets and peered around the white corner into the apartment. The walls remained empty and white in a neglect that was deliberate: Sidney decorated his apartment only with manuscripts. Copies of his dissertation rose in stacks from coffee table and end table, bar stools, counter top, white art-gallery pedestals, and the metal steps of a circular staircase that rose from the center of the apartment. A single armchair sat empty; the couch was covered in bed pillows and various small blankets.

Manuscripts and fine red dust. Sidney said this interior design decision was supposed to remind him to finish the work, but its only sure impact had been to drive him away, ever deeper into the little walk-in closet where he stared into the light of his computer screen, his back hunched, doing other things as the piles of manuscripts sat in sculptural array in what should have been his living space.

A rectangle of light poured out of the closet door, but no sound of typing broke the silence. Finally Paul just shouted.

"Hey Sidney!"

"Shh!"

"What? Why?"

"Ike's here."

"Ike?"

"The Wise Man. In the bedroom."

Sidney came into the living space and quietly gestured toward the closed archway of his bedroom door, as Paul whispered loudly behind him.

"Why is he here?"

"Sleeping."

There followed a silence that was characteristic of their friendship. Paul and Sidney were cogs in different machines. Finally, Sidney broke the silence with a whisper.

"Yesterday was disturbing a little, don't you think?"

Sidney pushed open a door to his patio and they walked outside, Paul reading the cover of a dissertation draft along the way.

"'*Falsetto Madness,* by Sidney Martin.'"

"Don't bring that up."

Sidney swung the door closed behind him, and they leaned against the railing and into the silence of Sunday morning. Paul squinted at his own apartment across the alley, trying without success to see through the windows ten or twelve feet away.

"So, what's the Vector gonna be this month, Mr. webmaster?"

No voice responded, and Paul turned his head. Sidney, too, was looking across the alley, but his eyes labored under heavy eyelids; their gaze seemed to lack the strength even to reach the windows, much less to assess their transparency or reflectiveness. Sidney should have been a foot taller than Paul, but his whole being sagged like the burden of the space he occupied: his shoulders, his chest, his brow, his eyelids seemed to hang from his spine.

Paul decided to persevere.

"What's the Vector you're working on, and what's it intersecting?"

"Youth."

"Why youth?"

Sidney's elbows found the iron banister and his weight shifted even further downward.

"What's youth intersect?"

Sidney cleared his throat.

"What torments me is that youth itself is beautiful. It torments me."

Paul smiled. "How melodramatic."

Silence.

"Are you afraid of being mistaken for a pervert?"

Sidney rose in response, pushing himself half an arm's length from the rail. He looked down at his feet, found a flattened cigarette butt with the tip of his shoe and dragged it through the dust of the patio concrete.

"No, Paul, it's not about sex. Everything isn't automatically about sex, Paul. I'm writing on the intersection of youth with beauty and of both with regret. Look, I think, uh... everyone can resist equating youth with sex, on at least some level. We've got that under control, and it's not a natural equation anyway. If you think about Darwin it really does make sense to have sex with people your own age, more or less. I told the Wise Man that late last night and he called me an imbecile—"

Paul laughed but Sidney did not hesitate.

"But I'm working on an explanation."

"Something to prove that aged men in Speedos and white tee-shirts don't naturally chase bikinis around?"

"If it's really important I can get someone to address the question of youth and sex and beauty. But the central problem is that youth itself is beautiful, in itself, and you never really get your finger on that until it's too late."

"Until you're too old to date teenagers."

Sidney returned his attention to the ground, and began an effort to push the cigarette butt into a drainage hole slightly above the level of the floor.

"You're being too limited. I'm not talking about teen lust. You can find plenty of that on the Web if that's what you like."

"I'm sorry. I was only kidding. Please don't make a site about teen—"

"It's teen beauty, man. The neon green of a new field of grass or new young emerging maple leaves. The explosive possibilities of a rosebud. But it's also about fear of death, on the other hand, especially here in this city where there is no concept of a life cycle. As you extrapolate it decays into a simpleton understanding of things, you know. Like life equals beauty and death equals ugliness. Something like that."

Paul wondered: if sex isn't involved, why does such beauty have to be regretted, and not just enjoyed? But, leaning over the banister to see into Sidney's face, he decided to drop the subject and let the Vector develop as it may.

"Did you sleep at all last night?"

"No."

Paul watched Sidney now, carefully, and waited for an explanation. He risked a guess.

"So. Youth Vector intersecting with beauty and regret?"

"Yes, Volume 24, Beauty; Regret, Volume 12; and Truth, Volume 1."

"They all intersect with Truth."

Sidney finally smiled and finished the cigarette-butt project.

"Yes, whether they're truthful or not."

Paul watched the little paper tube catch the wind and land on the second-floor patio just below. He looked back at Sidney.

"And kindness, the Vector of Kindness?"

For a moment Sidney traced his thumb along the curving iron rail of his patio.

"Kindness? Why do you say that?"

"I don't know. That was last week's Vector. You tend to—"

"Well I don't know if you could intersect youth and kindness."

A little pause came and Paul broke it.

"Oh, man, you're bitter."

"No. Regretful."

"By god, Sidney, you're only—"

"32, yes."

"If you regret now, you'll only regret it when you're older. You'll regret regretting."

"Yeah. I know."

"You'll get yourself into a vicious cycle."

"Yeah, I know."

"Hmm."

Sidney turned flat against Paul's face for the first time.

"Spry youth yourself. Fresh young optimist. You sound a little like old Ike in there."

Paul remembered the bearded old Wise Man.

"What's Ike doing here anyway?"

"I think he was kind of disturbed by the freeway experience yesterday. You know, he hasn't even left the Cornfields in, like, three months. He knocked on the door at nine o'clock; we sat up drinking tequila until four in the morning. I had to carry him to the bed and sleep on that couch."

Sidney smiled in satisfaction of the memory, and Paul happily slapped him on the shoulder.

"Ha! Like old confederates."

Sidney continued to smile but his body began to sag back toward the railing. Paul tried again to peer into his own apartment across the alley, looking for Sarah.

"So, couldn't he find Doc Bardot to fraternize with?"

"Evidently Doc's out somewhere on some jet. A big mythological private jet. Ike was speculating about it all night long."

"Hm."

Paul tried to imagine the interior of a private jet before continuing.

"He must be coming home today."

"Why?"

"He's having that big party tonight."

"That's tonight?"

"Yeah."

Paul ground some dust into the concrete floor with his own foot.

"I tell you, it's great to hear that you stayed up all night with a real person instead of people in the computer."

"People online are real. You always forget that."

Paul just smiled.

Sidney continued:

"Aren't I real, for instance, when I'm online?"

"Vector of Reality."

"I'm not ready for that one."

Sidney turned without another word and they went inside. He took two bowls from a kitchen cabinet and divided into them the remaining contents of a cereal box. He opened the refrigerator and held up a white carton. Half as wide as the usual milk thing, it was therefore some kind of soy or rice product.

"Uh, yes, please."

Paul received an overflowing bowl and a spoon and followed Sidney up the circular staircase that twisted from the apartment's geographical center. At the landing above was a wooden door that was almost ceremonial in its weight; but it opened to the usual bleak terrain of a flat rooftop: a floor of gravel and small detritus surrounded by low brick walls, punctuated by aluminum ventilation poles and inexplicable objects covered with tar. From this vast floor rose a dozen plaster north-facing rhomboids, each with its own heavy wooden door. Sidney grabbed and unfolded two chairs that leaned against his own rhomboid, and brushed them clean of terracotta-colored dust. Paul and Sidney sat next to one another, eating cereal and looking at the skyscrapers that rose from the neighborhood's uneven rooftops and the city's network of transportation arteries. Sidney raised his bowl in salute.

"Penthouse elegance."

"I wouldn't change a thing."

"Where's Sarah, anyway?"

"In our apto."

"Was she disappointed not to go to the wake?"

"She's used to it."

"She wasn't angry that you didn't have it somewhere closer?"

"She understood that we had to have it on the freeway."

"She did?"

Paul smiled.

"I know. She was alone in that too."

They ate their cereal, adding to the urban din the sounds of spoons and bowls and crunching and slurping. Paul's eyes traced the patterns and the harsh edges of the buildings, and he found himself overcome by a sense of wonder at the size of the undertaking. Even despite the millions of people and machines, and even despite the decades it had taken, and even despite the critical mass that perpetuates development when it occurs, it seemed impossible that something so elaborate and complicated could actually exist.

Sidney's voice brought him back.

"You loving her still, man?"

"Huh?"

"Sarah."

"Oh. Oh, yeah, absolutely."

"Good for you guys. Good for you guys."

3

Sarah, just awake, gazed into the grounds. She savored the coffee, the whole process: the smell of beans grinding, the texture of the rough powder, the pulverized dust underneath her fingernails. She poured a full and heaping lid into her round blackened steel machine, twisted the device closed, and set it on the flame. Sarah noted her reflection in the window above the sink, the tangled halo of her hair; she raised her eyebrows, smiled, and looked away.

Back on the counter, on the old cutting-board staging area, she had left a crescent-moon overflow of coffee powder, which, she noticed, had a surprising reflection of red. Was it the dark earthly cousin of the terracotta-red dust on the windowsill? With a single rotation of fingers, she dragged some of the powder into the cutting board, pressing it over and through. She brought her eyes closer and with the pad of her thumb ground a portion further, deeper into the wood. She brought the board up to the window at the level of her eyes to investigate the combination of tones, the native yellows of the board and the various depths of powder, the black and brown and curious red; the coffee deeply coloring and emphasizing the grooves and ridges of the wood.

And the results were not interesting, like in art school long ago when she had added a teaspoon of espresso powder to her paint medium. It only served to create a dark forgery of the patina of age, almost a mockery, like coffee spilled over paper to make an antique. Rubbing, with painful redundancy, an old piece of wood that possessed its own history: the years of cuts and soaking and cracks and the oils and sauces and spills of wine and chicken blood.

She rubbed the tip of her thumb against the inside of her lower lip, then carefully poured off the cutting board into the lid of the grinder. On the stove, a wisp of steam escaped from the steel machine as the heat and pressure began to push the water upward through the grounds and into the collector above. Sarah went and got a good mug.

She took her coffee into the living room where, next to her powerful desk, she had a small bed with a dozen or more pillows that converted it into a comfortable and handsome couch.

She pushed them off and took a sip of the coffee—

"Hot as hell!"

She set the cup on the floor and spread herself out on her back on the bed, letting her arms and the top of her spine and her head hang down under their own weight. Stretching her back and letting the blood flow into her head, she absently began to smooth out the tangles of hair with her fingers while consciously working on her sense of perspective in the upside-down room. The sloped white ceiling was its floor; the sun in the windows beamed in from below. An intimate familiarity with the upside-down was crucial for a designer.

Paul always laughed at this justification, but ritual was ritual no matter what he said.

From this vantage point, she had a full view of the up-side-down equipment under the desk and the two enormous computer monitors that reached forward, above, like two blank-faced gargoyles. They were dark now and perversely seductive.

Wait. She stopped herself. Were they really seductive? If they were, they seduced her like a factory rising from the mist seduces its approaching night shift. Out there, rising from the darkness and the mist, the factory's smokestacks appear distant and imposing; the vast building itself follows with its row of black dark windows, some of them broken, high along the roof line; and then the gate and the wide doors and then the time-cards. The workers' hands reach out and slam the cards in; and then the workers themselves enter the machine to pull in raw materials and push out products. But despite the nature of their presence, the monumental buildings and the smokestacks and even the factory equipment, impressive and shaming, serve as a second home, a place in which the workers exist among other people as humans, not to mention a reliable source of shelter.

Seductive was not the right word. The monitors were sustenance. They paid the bills. And they were the bills, coming up again, the computers and the monitors and the other tools there, and the student loans and credit cards and for god's sake the rent—her part of Paul's mortgage. She had to work, tear out all this hair to design book jackets, and, today, to make an advertisement for shoes out of nothing but two weak images and a paragraph of ad copy, the screechings of carnival barkers in polite society.

She extracted her fingers from her hair, twisted upright on an elbow, drank from her cup, and lowered herself upside-down again. Now she faced the high front wall with its windows and pictures framed in good design. Outside the sky was blue and the wall across the alley was brick; the opposite windows, Sidney's windows in fact, reflected back the roof line of her own apartment.

What a miracle is glass.

Factories, factories, factories. Pictures hanging, framed pictures, framed windows, stillness enabling, slowness; fingers ran through hair, massaging thoughts out, slowing thoughts down. Pictures and windows in frame.

The tops of two heads appeared in one of the frames, and then the face of Sidney and then of Paul, then the backs of their heads as the doors closed behind them. They approached the rail and stood talking. For a few long seconds Paul squinted helplessly into the glass. Was he trying to see her?

Paul. Was he trying to see a wider picture, the whole diorama box of their life together? Or was he just following the urge of the mystery-box: the fundamental human need to look inside something that is closed? In any case, he did not succeed, and his attention eventually turned to something on the floor of the porch.

Two men in design in the frame of an upside-down patio, in the frame of a building, in the frame of a window, moved and talked with animation. Paul stretched with good posture into the bottom of the frame; Sidney curled toward the viewer like a serpent hanging from a tree. He was a nice man, but distant somehow, concerned, cognitive. He pushed the edges of his mouth upward to make sure he was smiling. He had difficulty with eye contact; yet just now he seemed to be looking directly at her.

She closed her eyes for one last moment to think. Then she would exercise, and then she would work. It was Saturday morning.

Jesus Christs
Novel Excerpt
A.J. Langguth

God swept in while Christ was lost in daydreams. "Finished?" he asked peremptorily.

"Almost."

"You should be done by this time. I've told you it doesn't pay to hesitate. What have you got left—the floods?"

Christ spun the earth idly. "No, I put one there," he touched the globe, "and another up there."

"That looks all right." When he could do it honestly, God liked to sound encouraging. To himself, he wondered whether Christ would ever learn to work with speed and efficiency. To stir a harmless competition, he said, "Lamda has been done for hours."

"Lamda works with dust." Christ spoke indifferently.

"It means a great deal to him. He's spent time among those particles. In his way, he loves them, and his job is no easier than yours."

"I'm sorry."

"Why don't you finish quickly and join the others? What's holding you back today?"

"A broken spine."

"Is that all? Assign it now and come along with me. Do you have the list?"

He snatched the paper from Christ's hand and read through it rapidly. A good distribution on fires. I don't think I could have done as well." God moved his finger down the list again. "Here he is," he said. "Here's the man for the back." He shoved the papers back to Christ.

"Yes, I've seen his name."

"Then what's the delay?"

Christ spun the globe slowly between his knees and watched blurs of green and blue and occasional spots of yellow roll past his forefinger.

"If they didn't handle murder and war for themselves,"

God said reproachfully, "we'd have to get you a helper."

"I've heard from that man's wife," Christ said at last. "She calls every night."

"What does she want?"

"She doesn't want anything. She loves her husband and her family, and she calls to thank me for them. Even on busy nights she manages to get through."

God had begun paging through the book he carried everywhere. Its plain black cover was battered and some pages were dog-eared and stained. As a gift, they had presented him one year with a volume bound in green Florentine leather and indexed in gold. God had said the new book was far too handsome to use in his everyday work, and he had put it aside for some important occasion.

"Here they are," God said. "Married twenty-two years. Husband sustained minor wounds in a war. Son studying to be an engineer. Daughter with a minor talent for water colors." He slapped the book shut and confronted Christ. "Why shouldn't she give thanks?" he demanded. "What have they had to bear but his small nick in the shoulder and two cases of mumps?" He riffled through the pages of his book. "How many do you find like them?"

Defiantly Christ said, "Not enough."

"Not enough to make people slothful and weak," God said. "Not enough so that they forget how to handle adversity and death. How often I've told you, and how little you remember: I don't apportion sickness and storms because I enjoy their suffering. I don't do it to test their faith. I know the depth of a human being's faith, and I find no need to depress myself with new demonstrations."

"I remember that my performance depressed you."

"You were sent as a man. I didn't expect anything else. But these men and women of yours are going to die, and they have to be prepared for it. Can you imagine a life in which they passed from pleasure to pleasure, never failing in mind or body, until they were suddenly taken away. We must convince them of death's blessings, and sickness has proved to be our most persuasive argument."

"Must they die?"

God's anger never failed to intimidate Christ. "We'll let them live again as they once die, he said bitterly. "Two hundred, three hundred, five hundred years—until they come to hate the patterns of their lives and until the weight of repetition crushes them and until they choose death by the millions. We'll let you explain to them then why they had to keep on living after their will had gone and after breathing, the mere taking in of air, had become boring beyond their endurance."

"I forgot how it was."

"Look at you! Look at your own choice! Whenever you can, you hurry back here while your body is young and strong. You don't wait until age rots out your belly and shrivels your skin. One gray hair on your chest and you're back, away from the very people who are causing you such anguish today.

Christ nodded.

"They understand their fate better than you do," God continued. "Your miracles have become an embarrassment to them. They know they must bear the suffering they've been allotted, but they've become confused: to make you happy should they journey off to a cave and pray for health? Should they do that to prove their faith? Or should they stay at home, as their instincts tell them, and learn to live and die with their afflictions? You've muddled their thinking. I warned you, but your foolish sympathies led you astray."

"The healing was a mistake," Christ granted.

In a more kindly way, God said, "There's no point in going over all that again. Finish up now and meet me with the others."

"All right."

"If that woman doesn't call tonight, don't worry," God added as he was about to leave. "They'll be busy with him at the hospital. Then a shock sets in, and it might be a week or more. But from what you say, she'll get along. They're tougher than you remember."

When he had gone, Christ turned resolutely to the globe, checked out the coordinates and moved his marker to a microscopic dot in the middle of a continent. One jab, and he could cross the broken back off his day's list and hurry to join the others in the lounge.

That night Christ was sitting by the switchboard with a receiver in his hand when he heard the flat soft voice begin to speak. "I don't believe," she said, and even with the poor connection, Christ could hear her sniffle, "that we have the right to ask for health or money or happiness. Tom might not agree with me. You know he's never done much praying, and when he comes out of the anesthetic tonight, he might ask you for an end to his pain. You know what suffering can do to even a brave man.

"I'm not asking for courage, either. If I can do my part while he's in the hospital, it's because you gave me the strength long ago, and it's been inside me waiting to be used.

"Tonight I only want to thank you, as I have every other night, for giving me a man to love and children to take care of. This day was bad for us, but we have had many wonderful days, and I thank you as much for today as for any of the others."

Her voice faded, and Christ put down the receiver. The equipment had been built without speakers, and his answer to her stayed unspoken. "Don't take this," he would have said. "There was no cause. There was no reason. And whatever you do, don't thank me. You cannot offer thanks. I won't let you."

God found him sitting by the switchboard and put an arm around his shoulder. "I suppose she didn't call."

Christ looked at him through red-rimmed eyes. "She called," he said furiously. "She called and cursed us both. She hates you. She said she will never forgive you."

To Christ, God's smile looked hideous. "She will, though. She'll forgive me. You both will."

Editors' Note:
Jesus Christs, *originally published in 1968, was re-issued in 2003 by Figueroa Press.*

Coffee
A Novel in Progress
Nina Hiken

Ms. Lerner has to have more coffee. She has to; making it through a lesson without a cup of coffee nearby presents an agony not to be faced. Unfortunately, recess lasts just twenty minutes and in that time she can buy and drink only one cup. It is not enough.

She will sneak out of the classroom, leaving the children with an aide, a visiting parent, her room partner, anyone, so that she can get over to the cafeteria for one more cup. But they open only from 10 to 12:45 and, moreover, she knows this is a no-no; we never, ever, ever leave the children without certificated supervision during instructional time, no, no, no, no, no! A classroom of unattended children creates opportunity for paint in hair, petty theft, pee-pee in the pants, broken arms, scissors in the back, lawsuits, or at the very least a written reprimand for not teaching during teaching time.

She feels utterly abandoned. Why does she have to be the adult? Why does she have to be the one to make the lesson plans, to gather all the ingredients for the peanut butter balls, to clean out and cut open enough milk cartons for thirty-five bean plants? These kids can't do anything! They're so young and needy!

She has to have more coffee. Somehow, taking a sip of that hot, sweet, sugared liquid pacifies her. With the cup in her hand she is not alone. She wraps her fingers around her mug. The smooth ceramic glaze comforts her; the heat of the clay and the weight of it befriend her in this demanding world of Room 27 afternoon Kindergarten.

I had no idea that I felt that way. I only knew I needed something. So I drank about ten cups of coffee daily, ate heavy bran muffins on recess break, stuffed myself with three gummy worms for every one I passed out to a child, but couldn't find any soothing, couldn't get lasting relief from all my various angers and sorrows.

I was furious that I gave and gave to all my five-year old charges.

They came to me when no one wanted to be their friend, when they couldn't tie their shoes, when they couldn't build their castles or make a play dough dinosaur. No one in the District could be counted on to offer me what I had to provide unfailingly to them. I was utterly jealous of the fact that they had a caregiver, and I did not. This lack fueled my hatred for teaching, for the District, and for me. I had no idea that I felt that way. I only knew I needed ridiculous amounts of coffee.

Ms. Lerner needs her coffee. Finally, she gets an idea from Ms. B., the highly organized, slightly bitchy morning Kindergarten teacher in neighboring Room 26: Her own Mr. Coffee! Ms. B. has one on the paper towel dispenser above the sink. It even has a little quilted choo-choo train cozy cover matching the kiddie seat covers that she sewed over summer break.

This is brilliant, empowering, a thunderbolt, greater than Lincoln Logs or a new Madeleine story. Limitless coffee on demand. Yes, yes, yes! That very same afternoon she stops at a Lucky's supermarket. They have coffee makers. She buys herself a basic Mr. Coffee, a pound of French roast, some Coffee Mate, and a box of Sweet and Low. She would have bought sugar but it felt like a little too much indulgence.

The very next morning, about 7:30, Ms. Lerner joins her Kindergarten room partner, Mrs. K., in Room 27. She bounces in bright and early to set up the new comfort machine and still have time to run off the math copies.

"Hey, Mrs. K."

"What is it, hon?"

"I've got us a coffee maker. I thought I'd put it here, behind the plant on top of the towel dispenser. Is that okay?"

Mrs. K. didn't turn around. She was deep in bulletin board design, and had several pins in her mouth but she answered, "That's nice. We ought to be able to have a cup whenever, right?"

"That's what I thought. So is this an okay spot, here at the sink? I can't really think of another place that has an outlet in the right place."

"Oh, you know something, hon?"

"What?" asked Ms. Lerner, already anxious about the acceptance of the appliance installation.

"There seems to be, yes, I think there is, although it may have... gosh," said Ms. K. She finished taking down the jolly pumpkin poetry and began to arrange fat turkey poems on the wall. Talking to Ms. Lerner was a bit of a distraction from her primary task.

"There seems to be what?"

"Yes, I do think so… but then again, it could have changed, I don't know…"

"Mrs. K., what? What could have changed? What?" Ms. Lerner's Kindergarten partner, Mrs. K. always spoke slowly and thoughtfully; she took her time and deliberated as she shared her words. Sometimes a single idea took a full recess break to come out fully articulated. The young, coffee-drinking Ms. Lerner didn't have the time for this.

"She hates me. She is torturing me. This is way too passive-aggressive. I have got to get a new partner," decided Ms. Lerner. "What, Mrs. K.?" She squeezed the Mr. Coffee box to her chest.

I knew that Mrs. K. was actually a kind, deeply sensitive twenty-year teaching veteran and a breast cancer survivor who really needed and deserved all the time she took. She wasn't wasting time; she was savoring it. Every bit of time she had was precious; she used her minutes carefully. I just didn't want to give them to her, so great was my discomfort at finding myself twenty-eight years old, chubby, and a Kindergarten teacher without any romantic prospects.

"What are you thinking of, Mrs. K.," Ms. Lerner inhaled the aroma of Peet's French Roast. She tasted her first cup of coffee. She shifted her weight and hugged her Mr. Coffee.

"Well, there's a law, well, not a law, a rule, you know, something like that that says we can't have anything in the classroom that's dangerous to the kids."

"Really? But they have a coffee pot in the office."

"Well, you know how that goes."

"Well, it might be more dangerous to the kids if I don't have the coffee pot, you know what I mean?"

"Uh-huh." Mrs. K. went on pinning up giant construction paper turkeys and little poems about gobbling and being stuffed.

"Well, how about we keep it until they tell us not to? I mean, God! I want to be able to have a cup of coffee, you know, when it might not be recess break! And I want it to be good coffee! I got French roast!"

"Yeah, I know!" said Mrs. K., shaking a fat paper turkey in the air for the young unhappy Ms. Lerner.

"So you don't mind?"

"Gosh, no," said Mrs. K.

Ms. Lerner sighed a heavy breath. She unboxed the pot and set it over the paper towel dispenser, just like Mrs. B.'s. She stretched the cord along the splash guard at the back of the sink and reached the outlet under the wall-mounted, stainless-steel-framed kiddie mirror. The mirror, covered with tiny magenta tempera paint finger prints, caught her face as she bent down to plug in the cord.

Ms. Lerner looked at her self. She studied her face every chance she got. The 7:50 warning bell rang. She tucked her hair behind her ears. It was a good face, not a bad face at all. She saw thoughtful blue eyes, a funny nose, and a kissable mouth. She checked her flaws. Chipmunk cheeks, yes, a few zits, sure, and a terribly crooked hairline, but still... She stared at herself and thought, "There has got to be a man who would love this face. I know there has got to be." She took a lip gloss out of her pocket and spread it over her mouth.

The 7:55 start-of-school bell rang. I kept looking in the mirror. I didn't move.

You Have Such an Unusual Accent—Where Are You From?

Charles Kruger

I am from Grandma Bert who sang and danced in
    Vaudeville.
One night she warbled "When We Are M-A-Double-
    R-I-E-D
H-A-Double-P-Y we'll be" and burst out crying to my
    grandfather
Because they weren't yet. And Grandpa Sam who
    (after his stint in Vaudeville)
Ran a numbers racket when he learned that a short
    Jewish lawyer (who sang and danced)
Couldn't make much of a career even though he was
    Class President
And always voted Republican.
I emerged from the ocean at Craigville Beach in
    Hyannisport where
Great Grandma Lina brought peaches and plums to
    eat by the water.
I learned from Aunt Karyl who dyed her hair
    scandalously blonde
Laughed too loud, drank too much, and raised seven
    happy children
Before dying young and tired of pancreatic cancer.
I grew from Aura the schoolteacher, four feet ten
    inches tall.
Who once took a knife from a six foot student.
I was planted in the Mississippi mud, 1967, with
    Fannie Lou Hamer,
 "Ain't Gonna Let Nobody Turn Me Around," and
    "We Shall Overcome."
I am from alcoholic Grandpa Philip whom I never
    met.
And also the purple scent of lilacs and the yellow
    buzzing of bees.
I am from Nanny Annie who came to America
    speaking only Polish and Yiddish

But became a high school English teacher in less than
    two years.
I am from Aunt Helen who had her nose bobbed and
    never told her children about it
And Helen's daughter Susan who split into pieces,
    then came together again
Making two children before her final suicide attempt.
And Uncle Henry who taught me to do card tricks.
And I am from Pete who came to my door the night
    of his senior prom
To show off his powder blue tuxedo and took me on
    long humid summer drives
In his parents' Lincoln Continental.
I sprouted singing from the community theater
    where I once played
The Mayor of the Munchkins in the Wizard of Oz.
My queer accent is a fine new note in the family
    symphony.

The Man from Lloyd's
M.C. Gardner

Author's Note:

Thomas Stearns Eliot published The Waste Land *in 1922. In it, he explores the disillusion of the generation that survived the Great War and initiated the Jazz Age.*

The Man from Lloyd's *uses this poem and others by Eliot to dramatize his relationship with his first wife, Vivienne Haigh-Wood, and the memory of an impassioned friendship with Jean Verdenal, a French soldier killed in 1915. It also explores the ramifications conse-quent to a ménage à trois involving Eliot, Vivienne, and Bertrand Rus-sell during the First World War, and Vivienne's subsequent committal to Northumberland Asylum in July of 1938.*

The Waste Land *is divided into five parts: "The Burial of the Dead," "The Game of Chess," "The Fire Sermon," "Death by Water," and "What the Thunder Said."* The Man from Lloyd's *follows this plan and disperses these five sections over two acts. Lines from* The Waste Land *are numbered and italicized in the text of the play. Lines from other poems and plays are initialed and keyed to a note following the excerpts.*

After a brief prologue, the play opens in Eliot's office at the Lon-don publishing house of Faber and Faber, which is depicted as an arch and cathedral window fronting the Proscenium Scrim. It is January 4, 1965—the last day of Eliot's life. Eliot is told that the Man from Lloyd's has arrived for the "deposition." The Man from Lloyd's enters as a looming shadow projected on the Proscenium Scrim. Eliot invites him to sit and thereafter addresses the audience members as if they were the Man from Lloyd's. The Shadow will be seen again as the "electro-therapist" of Act 1 and as the "whip-master" of Act 2. The Man from Lloyd's is investigating a claim of conscience. He is a projection from Eliot's psyche—he is Death.

A pair of assassinations—of Archduke Francis Ferdinand and his wife in Act 1, and of John F. Kennedy in Act 2—bookends the play. In Act 1, Eliot imagines Bertrand Russell as the Serbian Assassin, Garvrilo Prinsip, and the murdered Countess as his own wife, Vivienne. In the first act Eliot's voice is highly Anglicized—it is a voice of subterfuge and denial. *In Act 2 his voice is more confessional, though remaining auricular. He imagines taking the sins of the world upon himself. Near the act's end, we find him staring down the sight lines of the single-bolt Mannlicher Carcano from the sixth floor of the Texas School Book Depository. We see the footage of the presidential motorcade projected behind the poet-assassin. Eliot's shots correspond with the carnage depicted on the screen. The final shot freezes and fades into history.*

During his final "confession" his accent will return to the more natural rhythm of his midwestern origins. Eliot's "mask," in Act 1, is the polished exterior he presented to the world. In Act 2 he applies makeup to a private, more interior face—the face of his doppelganger, Captain Colombo—the face of his death mask.

For D. Freed
"il miglior fabbro"

Scenes 4 and 5 are excerpted from the seven scenes of Act 1.

Act 1, Scene 4: The Urn

From the darkness a title card emerges on the Proscenium Scrim:

I. The Burial of the Dead

The title card fades. Scrim and Lights up. The dawn is frozen in the East. The ruin of a European cityscape is projected on the Rear Screen. The temple is suffused with the red and shadowed lighting of a wasteland. VIV *and* ELIOT *stand in the center of temple. They face forward. They address each other as if from separate worlds.*

VIVIENNE HAIGH-WOOD: Excuse me. I hope somebody knows where I am because my medicine is misbehaving.

T.S. ELIOT: It's not your medication.

VIVIENNE HAIGH-WOOD: Tom? You never came to that… "place"… in Northumberland. How is it I find you here? Where are we?

T.S. ELIOT: This was once a garden, Viv… where paradise was lost.

VIVIENNE HAIGH-WOOD: The trees are bare and the dead leaves stir across cracked earth.

T.S. ELIOT: Take care, Vivienne... the leaves are full of children—
(BN)

CHORUS OF CHILDREN (*v.o.*): Goosey, goosey gander, whither shall I wander? Upstairs, downstairs, in the fields I saunter.
(Repeat and fade behind dialogue.)

VIVIENNE HAIGH-WOOD: The children are hidden. They are the children the dead will never know. These are the children that we will never have.
(End nursery rhyme.)

VIVIENNE HAIGH-WOOD (*cont'd.*): I don't like your ancient garden, Tom. It makes me rather sad.
*(*VIV *deposits her cigarette in a Grecian Urn. The Urn is inscribed with a white rose. It is projected on the Rear Screen. The rose fades. She exits.* ELIOT *walks a few steps closer to his audience.)*

T.S. ELIOT (*to* MAN FROM LLOYD'S): My own vices aside—smoking, sometimes, has nothing to do with nicotine. Sometimes the poetry is deeper than the poem.
(The photograph of Jean Verdenal appears on the Rear Screen.)
(MUSIC CUE: Theme, "Sailor's Lament" from Wagner's Tristan und Isolde—more distantly afar.)

SAILOR (*recorded v.o.*): *Frisch weht der Wind.* (31) *Der Heimat zu.* (32)

T.S. ELIOT (*cont'd.*): Sometimes two together is more than twice alone—

VIVIENNE HAIGH-WOOD (*v.o.*): My nerves are bad tonight. Stay with me. Speak to me... why do you never speak? Speak! (111,112)

SAILOR (*recorded v.o.*): *Mein Irisch Kind* (33) *Wo weilest du?* (34)
*(*ELIOT *is frozen in place with his head cocked as if straining to hear the music through the recriminations. He picks up the Urn. He walks slowly, in a measured gait, to a pedestal at stage left. He places the urn on the pedestal. He returns short of breath and slightly bent. After each return from his narrative he appears more decrepit. He places his hand over his heart checking its palpitations. He speaks haltingly.)*

T.S. ELIOT (*to* MAN FROM LLOYD'S): Why does the day delay? *(Pause.)* When will time fly away? (FFE) Yes, there is a chill. *(Pause.)* Valerie, my second wife, assembled the ensemble I'm in: My morning coat and my collar mounting firmly to the chin, *(pause)* my necktie rich and modest but asserted with a pin. (LS)

(He exits. Scrim down. Darkness. Through the Scrim: Spot on the Urn ELIOT *placed on the pedestal, at stage left.* VIVIENNE *enters. She approaches and picks up the Urn. Its inscription is projected on the scrim beneath a white rose.)*

VIVIENNE HAIGH-WOOD ELIOT

*(*VIV *drops the Urn. Spotlight on* VIV *at center stage. She crouches in terror. She slams her fist against the floor.)*

VIVIENNE HAIGH-WOOD: No... Noooo... Dear God, Noooooo-ooo...

(A recorded chorus chants the word "burning" four times. Each repetition increases in ferocity.)

CHORUS: Burning, burning, burning, burning! (308)

(The scrim writhes with the red glow of projected fire. VIVIENNE *mimes the torture of the flame.)*

VIVIENNE HAIGH-WOOD: Ahhhhhhhhhhhhhhhhhhhh!

(She collapses. Darkness. Lights slowly up, center stage. ELIOT *cradles* VIVIENNE *at the foot of a plain wooden cross. She is unconscious. The pair is staged as a "Pieta."* ELIOT *prays through the shadows of the Proscenium Scrim.)*

T.S. ELIOT: O lord thou pluckest me out (309) O lord thou pluckest. (310)

CHORUS *(as if from afar)*: b-u-r-n-i-n-g... (311)

(Darkness. ELIOT'*s voice breaks in the darkness...)*

T.S. ELIOT *(v.o., in a sob)*: I tried to save her. Save her from the Pythagorean paganism of that pious, megalomaniacal, Godless prig!

(Lights up, Stage Left. ELIOT *is alone with the cross. Wearily, he removes his coat. He places it over an arm of the cross.)*

T.S. ELIOT *(cont'd. to* MAN FROM LLOYD'S*)*: Her hysteria always followed the failure of her flesh. I borrowed and begged to pay for medication. But her ailment was beyond medicinal application...

(A scarlet robe is lowered from above. He lifts it and holds it to his cheek.)

T.S. ELIOT *(cont'd.)*: Only the tattered Robe of Christ Jesus could stave off the certainty of her damnation. Only the Imperial Red of his chosen emissaries could deliver her from a darkness...

(Lights dim. A spot illuminates BERTRAND RUSSELL *in top hat, standing behind* ELIOT *and the cross—*RUSSELL *"lifts" the*

coat and exits to the wings.)

T.S. ELIOT *(cont'd.)*: ...growing in and with surety about her...
    (Darkness.)

Act 1, Scene 5: Peeping Tommy

The headline...

DULLES JOINS WARREN COMMISSION

...is projected on the Rear Screen. Lights up, center stage. Actor C,
MAURICE HAIGH-WOOD, *in military fatigues and officer's hat, and Actor*
D, BERTRAND RUSSELL *(in top hat) enter as a chorus with newspapers.*

MAURICE HAIGH-WOOD: The first thing to do is to form the
    committees— (C)
BERTRAND RUSSELL: Two pounds a week with a bonus as pretty.
    (C)
MAURICE HAIGH-WOOD: A commission has been appointed and
    bled— (C)
BERTRAND RUSSELL: The patsy has been anointed though dead!
        (They toss their respective papers in the trash and exit. ELIOT
        and VIVIENNE *enter at Stage Right and left.* ELIOT *wears
        the Imperial Red and Miter of a Cardinal. They each face
        forward. A coffin is illuminated between them.)*
T.S. ELIOT *(to* MAN FROM LLOYD'S*)*: The purported "sole"' assassin
    never stood alone. The undetermined prints on Oswald's
    rifle are our own.
VIVIENNE HAIGH-WOOD: Stay with me. Speak to me— (111,112)
T.S. ELIOT *(making the sign of the cross)*: Kyrie eleison, Christe
    eleison...
        *(*ELIOT *walks to the coffin. He pulls a black glove on his right
        hand.)*

DATE STAMP: 1-22-47
NORTHUMBERLAND ASYLUM
MORTUARY

VIVIENNE HAIGH-WOOD: Before the fires fed upon me, they put me
    in a box. At my back, in a cold blast I heard the rattle of

bones...

(ELIOT *takes hold of the raised lid of the coffin.*)

VIVIENNE HAIGH-WOOD: ...and chuckle spread from ear to ear as Tom... (185, 186)

(ELIOT *violently closes the coffin!*)

VIVIENNE HAIGH-WOOD *(cont'd.)*: ...latched the darkness down!

(The loud metallic clang, heard earlier in his office and at the seance, reverberates on the sound system.)

VIVIENNE HAIGH-WOOD *(cont'd.)*: We had no children—Tom didn't fancy them—unless you count the danseurs of the Ballets Russes. It's alright, Tommy... you can only properly kill a girl once.

(Darkness. Scrim down. Lights up on ELIOT under his office arch. ELIOT is still in his Cardinal Robes. He takes off his miter.)

T.S. ELIOT *(to MAN FROM LLOYD'S)*: What she meant? Vivienne was cryptic to the point of being elliptic. Yes, we talked of having a family. She wanted her first to be a girl. She bought a bolt of pink gingham from Chelsea and begged my mother for an heirloom lace that was nonpareil. A game that went too far? At the time I didn't see the harm in naming children born only in her mind. I had my verse... she had poetry of her own. We finally settled on a name. Yes, Marina. How did you know? That's right, Marina after Shakespeare's Pericles. Quite the only thing of value in the play. "What seas, what shores, what grey rocks and what islands, what water lapping bow and scent of pine and the woodthrush singing through the fog. What images return. O my daughter..." (M)

(ELIOT takes off his glasses. He appears diminished by a memory. He brushes tears from his eyes. A Confessional Screen is lowered from above. He puts the miter back on his head. Enter VIVIENNE, on opposite side of screen. He is her confessor. They both sit.)

VIVIENNE HAIGH-WOOD: Forgive me, Father. I am newly wed, but Tom and I sleep in different beds. He rarely comes to me. Marriage is not what I thought, not what I thought at all. I married Tom in Summer... I betrayed him in the fall.

(ELIOT stands and begins nervously pacing back and forth like a trapped animal.)

VIVIENNE HAIGH-WOOD: The blood upon the sheets suggested that

I was touched by more than I should know...

(VIVIENNE *begins to titter, hysterically.*)

VIVIENNE HAIGH-WOOD *(cont'd.)*: Bertie said he wasn't bothered by my menstrual flow.

T.S. ELIOT: Ahhhhhhhhhhhhhhhhhhhhhhhhhhhhhhhhhhhhhhhhhhhhh hhhhhhhhhhhhh!

(VIVIENNE *is startled by the violence of the scream. She takes a step or two back. She puts her hand to her mouth in fear.* ELIOT *regains his composure. He returns to the demeanor of a father confessor.*)

T.S. ELIOT *(to* VIVIENNE*)*: Child-Daughter, the "Marys" are sufficient to the day. Sin no more and go thy way...

(VIVIENNE *exits. Confessional Screen up.*)

DATE STAMP NOV. 22, 1921
DR. ROGER VITTOZ, PSYCHOLOGIST

(VIVIENNE*'s voice is heard on the sound system.*)

VIVIENNE *(v.o.)*: It's time, Tom—that's a good lamb...

(*Proscenium Scrim down.* ELIOT *sits facing the audience. He sits in the rigid pose of Francis Bacon's "Pope Innocent X" portraits. Enter* BERTRAND RUSSELL *(Actor D in top hat). He straps* ELIOT *to the chair.* ELIOT*'s fingers dance nervously on the ends of the chair arms. The shadow of the* MAN FROM LLOYD'S *looms upon the scrim. He speaks with* ELIOT*'s voice.*)

MAN FROM LLOYD'S (ELIOT*'s recorded voice*): Let's see. It says here that you wedded her in June and Russell bedded the remains. Is that accurate?

T.S. ELIOT: I wooed her, I won her and then the Devil came...

(*On the Proscenium Scrim, the* MAN FROM LLOYD'S *pulls a switch. Lights dim. We hear the crackle of electricity.* ELIOT *bolts upright in* VITTOZ*'s "electric chair."*)

T.S. ELIOT: Ahhhhhhhheeeee!

MAN FROM LLOYD'S *(suppressed amusement)*: Hmmm. It would appear that your betrothal and her betrayal... Why, they scarcely missed a beat—

T.S. ELIOT: It was then that the voices rose and started to repeat.

(*The* MAN FROM LLOYD'S *turns up the voltage. Lights dim. The electrical sound is louder.* ELIOT *strains against the teeth-shattering current.*)

T.S. ELIOT: Ahhhhhheeeeeeeeeeeeeeeeeeeeeeeee!

MAN FROM LLOYD'S *(recorded v.o.)*: Whispered they of good or whispered they of ill?

T.S. ELIOT: The only word they whispered was to KILL! To KILL! To KILL!

> *(On the Proscenium Scrim, the* MAN FROM LLOYD'S *administers a final blast of "therapy." The lights dim. Electricity arcs above* ELIOT*'s head. Smoke and sparks fly out from the bottom of the chair.* ELIOT *is, again, jolted upright in his chair...)*

T.S. ELIOT: Ahhhhhhhhhhhheeeeeeeeeeeeeeeeeeeeeeeeeeeeeeeee eeeeeeeeeeeeee!

> *(He grips the arms of the chair and strains upward mirroring the iconography of Bacon's "Screaming Pope" series. The* MAN FROM LLOYD'S *turns off the voltage.* ELIOT *slumps unconscious in his chair. Darkness.)*

VIVIENNE *(from the darkness)*: All done, Tommy—you'll soon be right as rain...

> *(Lights up.* BERTRAND RUSSELL *unfastens the straps on the chair. He pinches* ELIOT*'s cheeks. He passes smelling salts under the poet's nose.* ELIOT *twitches and slowly revives. He stands and painfully removes the Cardinal Robes and Miter. He hands the costume to* BERTRAND RUSSELL. RUSSELL *exits.* ELIOT *walks forward to a glass of water. He drinks and seems to regain a measure of strength. He continues his deposition with the* MAN FROM LLOYD'S.*)*

T.S. ELIOT *(v.o.* TO MAN FROM LLOYD'S*)*: The costume? Yes, Murder In The Cathedral. I didn't think Vivienne would mind. They both knew that I knew. They believed I was inclined.

> *(A clock chimes.* VIVIENNE *enters. She holds a whip. With each crack of the whip,* ELIOT *becomes increasingly agitated.)*

VIVIENNE HAIGH-WOOD: So you've been peeping. *(Crack of whip.)* Bloody peeping Tommy. I know something of death, Tom—courtesy of lessons learned in lockup. *(Crack of whip.)* You fuck with death and it will damn well fuck with you. Now that I'm dead I must live with my sins, whatever depth or depravation. *(Crack of whip.)* If it's any consolation, Bertie's caresses were unreproved if undesired. His hands encountered no defense. His vanity required no response and made a welcome of indifference—much like your own— (237, 238, 239, 240, 241, 242)

> *(Vivienne cracks the riding stock. The sound of the whip allows a little of the repressed Captain Columbo to break through.* ELIOT *slaps on his Stetson. He thrusts his hips forward miming a fevered rut.)*

T.S. ELIOT / CAPTAIN COLUMBO: She jack-knifed upward at the knees then straightened out from heel to hip pushing the framework of the bed and clawing at the pillow slip! (SWE)

> *(*ELIOT *stops abruptly. He removes hat. He is shamed in the gaze of the* MAN FROM LLOYD'S. *He continues, sickened at his display and the memory of the ménage à trois.)*

T.S. ELIOT *(cont'd.)*: ...and I would sit at the foot of the stair and flog myself until I bled—there would not be a word to say. You would love me because I should have strangled you— (Sebastian)

VIVIENNE HAIGH-WOOD: And I should love you the more because I mangled you. (Sebastian)

T.S. ELIOT: Vivienne, please!

> *(She sits. She lays out her Tarot.)*

VIVIENNE HAIGH-WOOD: Tom, Bertrand carries something on his back which I was forbidden to see. (56, 53, 54)

> *(She turns over the last card and gasps.)*

VIVIENNE HAIGH-WOOD *(cont'd.)*: Tommy, he's the one-eyed merchant! (52)

> *(Lights out.)*

First Reading of *The Man from Lloyd's:*

Valdelavilla, Spain
October 25, 2003
Director, Greg Stanford

Act 2, Scene 2: The Euminides

From the darkness a title card emerges on the Proscenium Scrim.

III. The Fire Sermon

Lights up on ELIOT *under his office arch. He is hunched forward. He uses his umbrella to support himself.*

T.S. ELIOT *(to* MAN FROM LLOYD'S): What is the old dictum? "A man can surely do what he wishes to do but he cannot determine what he wishes." I tried to control the disparate voices... they split me asunder. Their chaotic din was the cacophony of sin...

> *(Enter* VIVIENNE. *She speaks facing the audience—an embodied memory.)*

VIVIENNE HAIGH-WOOD: My nerves are bad tonight. Yes, bad! (111) Tom, I need a weekend by the sea...

> *(MUSIC CUE: Gotterdamerung Act 3 Scene 1. The* RHINEMAIDENS' *Theme is interfused with a fugue of conflicting voices. It is played behind the dialogue and enters in more fully as indicated.)*

RHINEMAIDENS (*recorded v.o.*): Weialala leia Wallala leialala... (276, 277)

> *(MAURICE (Actor C) and* RUSSELL *(Actor D) join* VIVIENNE *(Actor B). They surround* ELIOT *(Actor A) with their "chaotic din" spoken out to the audience.)*

BERTRAND RUSSELL (*actor D*): Here we have it—the key to Tourquay.

VIVIENNE HAIGH-WOOD: Is it proper, Tom? I'll be alone with him for half the holiday.

T.S. ELIOT: He's a trusted friend on whom we do depend.

BERTRAND RUSSELL: By the sea beneath a cliff, I'll do her in a rented skiff!

RHINEMAIDENS (*recorded v.o.*): Weialala leia... allalala. (290)

VIVIENNE HAIGH-WOOD: Highbury bore me. Richmond and Kew undid me. For Richmond I raised my knees supine on the floor of his narrow canoe— (294,295)

BERTRAND RUSSELL: What's a little blood between friends?

MAURICE HAIGH-WOOD (*actor C*): Goonight, Bertie —

RHINEMAIDENS (*recorded v.o.*): Wallala leialala… (291)

T.S. ELIOT: I came upon the sylvan scene, the change of Philomel, by the barbarous king, so rudely forced… (99)

VIVIENNE HAIGH-WOOD: After the event he wept. He promised "a new start." I made no comment. What should I resent? (297,298,299)

MAURICE HAIGH-WOOD (*actor C*): Goonight, Viv.

RHINEMAIDENS (*recorded v.o.*): Wallala leialala… (291)

BERTRAND RUSSELL: Please, Tom… use the flat at your leisure…. I'll tend to your wife, at her pleasure.

T.S. ELIOT: And still she cried. (103)

VIVIENNE HAIGH-WOOD: What are you thinking of? What thinking? What? I never know what you are thinking. (113,114)

RHINEMAIDENS (*recorded v.o.*): Weialala leia… (277)

T.S. ELIOT: I think we are in rat's alley where the dead men lost their bones. (115,116)

MAURICE HAIGH-WOOD: Goonight, Tom. He's a good man, Viv.

VIVIENNE HAIGH-WOOD: He's a good man, Maurice. Goonight, Tom.

BERTRAND RUSSELL: He's a fine lad. Top of his class. Hats off, hats off to Thomas Stearns Eliot!

(*Actors, B, C, and D jeer and cheer the despondent poet.*)

MAURICE HAIGH-WOOD: Goonight!

T.S. ELIOT: Noooooooooooooooooooooo. Stop time! Stop… stop…

(*He collapses to the floor. The Rhinemaidens stop singing.*)

T.S. ELIOT (*in a shattered whisper*): Time to stop…

(*Darkness. A sobbing is heard in the dark. Lights slowly up. ELIOT is alone on the floor. He looks about in a private terror. His mind becomes increasingly unhinged in his confession to the MAN FROM LLOYD'S.*)

T.S. ELIOT (*to MAN FROM LLOYD'S*): What place is this? What quarter of the world? (M) The Russell affair? (*Coughs.*) Yes, there was pain enough to be enjoyed by all. Bertie was a wolf, indeed, but the wolf in bed with "Little Red" was my private letch and wretched scheme! Ha! Ha! Now there's a tale as grim as any found in Grimm or in God's "Good Book," grey and grand! Russell was a god and "Mary" was his maid—but my Vivie was no virgin, no Catholic should complain. I put the two of them together—we made a trinity of sin. They fell deep into perdition because I pushed them in! Ha! Ha!

(Howling of the hellhounds. ELIOT *looks furtively about in increasing dementia.)*

T.S. ELIOT: Listen... listen to my pretties. You don't see them, you don't—but there's no rest from them. The Eumenides are always close at hand or hem. Heel, ladies! Bastards all—Listen... You can hear their fervent scratching... Take heed, take heed—the bitches mount the wall!

(Loud growling and barking on the sound system. ELIOT *falls to his knees and puts his hands above his head as if trying to expel the imminent attack of the leaping hellhounds.)*

T.S. ELIOT: Ahhhhhhhhhhhhhhhhhheeeeeeeeeeeeeeeeeeeeeeeee eeeeeeeeeeeeeeeeeeeeeeee!

(Darkness.)

Note on the Masks:

Masks facilitate the multiple identities of the four cast members. Eliot dons a blackface minstrel mask for his rendition of "My Mammy." The Man from Lloyd's wears the identical mask for "Toot, Toot, Tootsie Goodbye." Eliot and Russell wear wolf masks, wolf tails, and wolf claws during their "Top Hat" number. Each of these masks will be cut out around the face and chin to allow full vocal resonance. The only "realistic" masks are those of JFK and Marilyn Monroe—worn near the conclusion of Act 1.

Note on the Hats:

Headgear further differentiates the characters. Eliot and the Man from Lloyd's wear identical Bowler Hats. Eliot's doppelganger "Wild Cat" Colombo wears an oversize Stetson. Bertrand Russell favors a Top Hat. Maurice Haigh-Wood always has his Petty Officer's Hat near hand or head. Actor B, Vivienne/Valerie, covers her head with a black Mourning Shawl at the play's conclusion.

Note on Gunshots:

Three distinct concussions are employed. The gunshot connected with the death of Jean Verdenal echoes in the distance as if remembered in a dream. The gunshots that fell the Archduke and his wife issue from a silencer; the impacts are low-decibel, sickening thuds. The three shots

Set Sketch: The "ruin" of Eliot's childhood home

that close Act 1 and that repeat at the Kennedy assassination, near the end of Act 2, are of increasingly louder volume until the final shot of each is a deafening concussion.

Note on the Music:

In *The Waste Land,* Eliot quotes from two of Wagner's operas: "The Sailor's Lament," from Act I of *Tristan und Isolde* and "The Rhinemaidens Chorus," from Act III of *Gotterdammerung.* These will be operatically vocalized from recordings. Jean Verdenal was a fan of both these operas. Eliot dedicates *Prufrock and Other Observations* to his doomed friend: "For Jean Verdenal 1889-1915 *mort aux Dardanelles.*" The Rhinemaidens of Wagner's *Ring Cycle* emerge as the mermaids of Eliot's *Prufrock.*

Eliot was a contemporary of Al Jolson. The music of the Cantor's son is used in five scenes. The play opens with Jolson's "April Showers." Eliot courts Vivienne with medley of "I'm Sitting on Top of the World / Baby Face." He later remembers his mother with a hybrid rendition of Berlin's "My Mammy." Eliot joins Vivienne in a duet of "After You've Gone Away." The surviving characters salute the poet with the music hall standard, "Toot, Toot, Tootsie, Goodbye."

Set Sketch: Eliot's office at Faber & Faber

Key to Lines Incorporated in the Play:

Ariel Poems
    Marina (M)
Ash Wednesday (1930) (Aw)
Captain Columbo **
The Cocktail Party (Cp)
The Family Reunion (Fr)
Four Quartets
    Burnt Norton (Bn)
    East Coker (Ec)
    The Dry Salvages (Ds)
    Little Gidding (Lg)
The Hollow Men (1925) (Hm)
The Jolly Tinker (JT)**
The Love Song of Saint Sebastian (Sebastian)**
Minor Poems
    Five-Finger Exercises (Ffe)
    Lines for an Old Man (Lom)
Murder in the Cathedral (Mc)
Poems (1920)
    Gerontion (G)
    Burbank with a Baedeker: Bleistein with a Cigar (B)
    Sweeny Erect (Swe)
    Whispers of Immortality (W)
    Sweeny among the Nightingales (Swn)
Prufrock (1917)
    The Love Song of J. Alfred Prufrock (Ls)
    Preludes (P)
    Rhapsody on a Windy Night (R)
    Mr. Apollinax (A)
Unfinished Poems
    Sweeny Agonistes (Swa)
    Coriolan (C)
The Waste Land (1922) Lines 1 – 434
    Preface (Wlp)
    Notes (Wln)
    Edit (Wle)

In Appreciation and Acknowledgment
of
The Complete Poems and Plays
1909–1950 *
of
Thomas Stearns Eliot

---

* © 1952, Harcourt, Brace & World, Inc., New York.

** "The Jolly Tinker" (JT) and "Captain Colombo" verses were not included in any collections authorized by the poet. They survived in Ezra Pound's papers collected at the Beinecke Rare Book and Manuscript Library, Yale. "The Love Song of Saint Sebastian" (Sebastian) is pre-Prufrock and not in the standard collection.

Blind Date
A Novel in Progress
Stephanie Silberstein

Grandma won't like it: I'm taking Todd on the Ferris wheel tonight. I'm still staring at the closet.

Creak… pull… turn. Grandma. Jump up T-shirt over head door cracks open. "Katherine…" I head out, Grandma comes in. Her eyes slide down me, T-shirt to jeans. My hair… brush it… still a mess. Hand over brush, fall back on bed.

Grandma's eyes shine. She pushes, I'm up. "Where…" Head down hair in eyes. "…dressing so fancy?" Streaks in carpet. "Carnival." A knot. Grandma tugs. Head bounces, up, down, up. I'm dizzy. Look in mirror. "So what's this Todd like?" Tangled clump. Grandma tosses it. "Haven't seen him since mom got sick." Tug, twist. She lowers her voice—afraid house is spying on us. "He's been lonely…" Twist, pull. "…living up at Bloomfield." Bulletin board's empty—took down rejections. "A college boy?" Pull, twist, tug. "Like it?" Rub head stare at reflection. Neat half-braid. "It's OK." Grandma's lips thin. "Take a sweater." I go across. Grandma's hair. Soft. Tap-tap-tap. My laces. Grandma stares. My shoes. Tie them. "You'll catch cold."

Run—jump down steps. Grandma's shadow meets wall. Grab banister, turn, run back up, knock photo off desk.

Closet's dark. Reach in, squeeze air, rub face into fabric 'til I sneeze. Grab something. Snap! Hanger falls, neck broken. Dive for the sweater, put it on, kick the hanger into darkness. Another creak, another knock. Light, the hall, Grandma. Flip braid over shoulder, wave, walk away. Hold head high, but take dinky steps to the door. Slam. I run. Stand on the sidewalk, throw back my head, taste the wind 'til I've had enough.

I get in my car, roll the window down, and drive away, singing. "I'm With You."

There's a line to park. I fiddle with the knobs on my radio. Just static. Speed into the lot. My brakes squeal. Back up, watch the smog coming out of the other guy's car. He goes, I take the space. I roll up the window before I head for the grounds. You never know who might be hanging around.

Rusty fence by the Ferris wheel. I lean back, squeeze a spike. Shade my eyes with my hand as I look around.

A boy. Todd? He's whistling, squinting, coming this way. I step towards him. He turns away, stuffs his hands in his pockets. The spike burns as I slide my hand down. Wait… he's coming back. He's grinning. "Katherine?"

I nod. He holds out his hand. Fingers long, skin smooth, nails even. "I'm Todd. Obviously."

I sandwich his hand between my two. He steps back and I let go.

"C'mon, let's get hot dogs." Todd heads for the food court.

I look over my shoulder. Ferris wheel's the other way. My stomach growls. I won't eat, though. I don't want to get sick.

We're near the front of the lines when I ask, "Have you ever seen so many people?"

Todd beckons me forward. "Two hot dogs, one with relish and mustard, and…" I shrug. Todd orders me a plain dog. I have two bucks waiting, but he shakes his head. I crumple them into my pocket. Tiny boxes appear on the counter. Todd takes one for me. "No, I haven't." He smiles. His teeth, large and white, fit his mouth. "This is the first time I've ever been to a fair, actually."

Picnic area's too crowded. Todd dives in, weaves between little kids. I look around, bite into my dog. Three kids playing rock, scissors, paper. A lady taking over a whole table. Is that guy leaving? No.

Empty grass behind the tables. "How about here?" Todd asks.

"We don't have a blanket."

Todd sits down anyway. I rub my shoe against the grass. Dry. I can sit here.

My hot dog's gone. I toss the box. It flutters away. The wind plays with Todd's hair. My hand goes to his knee. He pushes it off.

I put my hands in my lap and squeeze. "Sorry." Todd stares into space, says nothing. Wipe, wipe, wipe… fingers clean now. He still won't talk.

"So… how do you like Bloomfield?"

Todd squashes his box into a ball. He tosses it. It flies towards the trash, hits the rim. "C'mon. Roller coaster's waiting."

I stand up, squint. Roller coaster snakes around its track. I twist my head 'til I'm dizzy, following it. "I'd rather not."

Todd rolls his eyes. "My stomach can't take fast rides," I say.

"Oh. Well, let's go on the baby coaster then and see how you do."

I take a few steps the other way. Lights flash on and off, calling me. I make myself turn around. "Don't you have to be, like, less than four feet tall in order to go on that?"

Todd's eyes X-ray me. "Oh, you could pass for a little girl, no problem." The probes sparkle. "No more excuses. C'mon!" He runs. I follow him. I have to.

I watch the baby coaster for about two seconds. Some kid cries. The operator pulls a lever to stop everything. I trace the shadow of his muscles. The line moves up. I flash him a smile.

Todd brushes my fingers. His hand ducks behind his back as I turn.

The ride stops then. Todd tiptoes forward. "Hi." He stares someplace far away. I nudge him. "Tickets." Todd grins. Rip. Two tickets off our roll, into the guy's hand.

I push the turnstile. Hard. Todd follows me through. I reach for his hand. "Let's get the front car." Todd's hands disappear into his pockets again. I skip to keep up with him. In the car I pull the safety bar down first thing. Second thing, I put my arm around him.

Todd slides away. He studies Lever Guy. "So that's how they run this thing."

"Yeah," I say. "One time the Ferris wheel guy wasn't paying attention and I went around forty times. It was like having my own private space." I slide my hand down Todd's back.

Todd pats my other hand. "This ride OK on your stomach, Katherine?" My eyes sting. "If I have to I'll lean over the side." I fake a cough and Todd pats my back. Crash, jerk, bump. Ride stops. Chest hits safety bar, it lifts up. Don't wait, run. Swish, swish

—my jeans.

Lock won't close. Twist, pull, tug—clicks shut. On my

knees, sobbing. Toilet water ripples.

I stand up, look in the mirror. Eyes too puffy—rinse. Tighten braid, go out.

Todd's waiting for me. "Katherine."

I go flat against the wall. Todd keeps coming.

"Look," he says. His eyes are large and round. "I'm sorry the baby coaster didn't agree with you. Wanna try something else before calling it a night?" I reach for his hand but get freaked and don't take it. "Like what?"

"You choose."

My tongue taps my teeth. "The Ferris wheel, then."

We walk across the grounds, together but not together. My hands hang loose at my sides; Todd's stay in his pockets. At the Wheel, I lean on the fence. I swallow. Lights slide, calling me again.

We get inside. Just us two. The guy locks us in. I lean back as he hobbles to his lever. The car rises. "So where do you go to school?" Todd asks.

I press my nose against the window. A lady in a big hat matching a toddler's. The baby shuffles its feet. "I don't." Todd looks out, too, avoiding me. "I do web design. Someday I'm going to have my own business."

"Wow! How'd you ever tell your parents?"

Last spring. Mom was gone two months. I got the last rejection. Grandma took me to Swanson's. She made me have a sundae with everything. The hot fudge tasted bitter. I wanted to be alone. "It just sort of happened," I say.

Todd nods. It's quiet 'til the car stops mid-air. It swings back and forth. He says, "I don't know what I'm in school for." He grins. "Maybe I'll drop out."

I grab the handrail. It's cold and hard. "Oh, no, don't!"

Todd rocks the car. "Look at that view."

The car rises again. I'm dizzy. I kneel at the window. Lights sparkling, moving, sliding. On the rides, the midway, the freeway: buzzing... singing... calling me.

Car stops, swings. Across the grounds, lights flip upside down, never go out. Push hard at window—car jerks, moves. I'm sinking, sinking. Past the freeway, past the lights. I kneel at the window. The light-riders scream.

Scrape. The Ferris wheel lands. Ride's over.

Loki Saves the Hammer
A Puppet Play
Leon Katz

Scene 1

VOICE: Thor, the God of War,
    With his wild red beard and his eye
    As bright and as fierce as fire,
    Chortles and laughs and grins
    As he tosses his hammer in air.
The gods live snug and secure
    In Asgard, heavenly home,
    Protected by him, by Thor
    And his magic hammer which flies
    Over the gates and the walls,
    And believe it or not flies back
    Of its own accord to the hand
    Of merry and terrible Thor.
Each time it flies from his hand
    And travels who knows where,
    A cry of pain is heard
    From the mouths of the enemy.
    Jotuns, they're called, the giants
    Who in the dead of night
    Creep and crawl to the walls
    To the very gates of the gods,
    Trying to pillage and burn,
    To destroy the heavenly home,
    Longing to win for their envious selves
    Heavenly majesty.
But the magic hammer of Thor
    Unerringly finds each one
    Wherever the jotun is hid
    And flies to his hiding place
    And neatly chops him in two.
    And at every hammer's thud
    And at every jotun's scream,
    The mighty God of War
    Slaps his thigh with delight

And sends the hammer for more.
And so morning, noon and night,
   He gleefully does his chore
   Relishing every kill
   That keeps gods and heaven secure.
   But deep in the night, he yawns,
   Fatigued by the fun of the day.
   With a belch and contented sigh,
   He lies down to sleep and snore.
One beautiful Asgard morn,
   Loki as usual comes
   To bring him his morning meal—
   Loki, half-giant, half-god,
   Gnashing his teeth that he,
   Of all the demi-gods,
   Is chosen to drag the cart
   Loaded with pots of mead,
   With the carcasses of two cows,
   And a giant net full of fish,
   To slake the mighty thirst
   And bolster the mighty strength
   Of the waked-up God of War.
He gingerly taps the arm
   Of sleeping, snoring Thor,
   Knowing it's wiser by far
   To favor the little tasks
   That win the friendship and trust
   Of Thor and the other gods,
   All of whom always, ever,
   Despise and are wary of him,
   Whose cunning and tricks they like
   When they serve, but when they do not,
   They give them the godly pip.
So setting the mounds of food,
   He wakes the mighty Thor,
   Who stretches, belches, and roars,
   And grabbing a pot of mead,
   He reaches with one hand
   For the hammer, his love, his delight.
   He reaches, and reaches, but lo!
   It is nowhere; the hammer is gone!

THOR: It's gone!

LOKI: Gone?!

THOR: Gone!

LOKI: Impossible!

THOR: It's gone! Look for yourself!
    It's gone!

VOICE: Gone, the hammer is gone.
    But while Thor is tearing his hair
    And roaring with pain and chagrin,
    Cunning Loki considers:
    Who has the skill and the guile
    And the dare and the wit to creep
    Silently in the night,
    And from under the sounding nose
    Of terrible Thor snatch up
    The magical hammer and steal
    Away, unseen and unheard?
    Who? Only one! King Thrym,
    The King of the Jotun hoard.

LOKI: He alone has the guile
    And the wit to do this thing.

THOR: Who? Never mind! Whoever.
    Loki, my friend, my dear!
    Find him, find him, before
    Those Jotuns, those devils, discover
    The magic hammer is lost,
    And gather in force to attack,
    And destroy our heavenly home.

VOICE: And Loki, knowing the gods
    Will be grateful to him forever
    For saving their heaven and home,
    Goes off to recover the hammer.

Scene 2

VOICE: Massively beautiful Freya,
    The love and the pride of the gods,
    Her beauty outweighing them all,
    Wonder of wonders, travels
    On golden falcon wings
    Which lift her, wonder of wonders,
    Into the air at a clip,

And bear her to distant places
In less than the wink of an eye.
FREYA: My wings!
LOKI: Your precious wings.
FREYA: And what will you do with them?
VOICE: But Loki, sworn to tell no one
The what and the why of his trip,
Begs the magnificent Freya
To trust in his need and give—
FREYA: Trust? In Loki the liar,
The thief, half-Jotun, half-god?
Madness!
VOICE: And laughing and laughing
Her corpulent golden laugh,
She bodily elevates Loki
And pitches him out of the room.
But desperate Loki, needing
Desperately her wings,
Scrambles back to her side,
And ducking the swing of her arm,
Whispers into her ear
The news of the theft of the hammer,
And the danger it holds for the gods.
Virginal Freya, seized
By fear for the ruin of heaven
And the twilight of the gods,
Lets flow from her sky-blue eyes
A stream of golden tears,
Rips the wings from her shoulders,
And claps them onto the back
Of anxious, trembling Loki,
Spins him around to face her,
And whispers urgently:
FREYA: Take these wings and fly
To the land of the Jotun beasts.
VOICE: And slipping a golden bracelet
From off her capacious arm,
She adds with a tearful smile:
FREYA: Bring back the magic hammer
And I will reward you with this.
Come back empty handed,

And I will tear you limb from limb.
VOICE: Needing no other urging,
    Loki takes off on wing.

Scene 3

VOICE: Flying, flying, he skirts
    Lightning and thunder clouds,
    But flocks of angry geese,
    Alarmed and enraged at the sight
    Of a demi-god with wings,
    Cackle and nip at his heels,
    And Loki, in godly terror,
    Circles and zooms, and at last
    Escapes from the menacing fowl,
    And reaching Jotunheim,
    There! On the top of the mountain,
    He sights the Jotun castle
    Where Thrym, the King of the Jotuns,
    Lives with his army of giants,
    Secure in his castle eyrie,
    Impregnable from without.
  Loki alights on the ramparts,
    And Thrym, half-cousin, half-foe,
    Greets the traveler warmly,
    Grinning from ear to ear.
    Why is he grinning? thinks Loki.
LOKI: Aha, my suspicion is right!
THRYM: Suspicion? Suspicion? Dear Loki,
    What is there to suspect?
LOKI: Hm.
VOICE: Says Loki.
THRYM: Come,
    Come, sit!
VOICE: Says Thrym with a grin.
VOICE: They sit, they gorge, they guzzle,
    They chat of this and that,
    Both thinking nothing but: hammer,
    Neither mentioning it.
    Loki at last, in a fog,
    Crammed full of food and wine,
    And ready to fall asleep,

Rouses himself to mention
A tidbit—news of the day—
Something about a hammer,
The hammer of, well, of Thor.

THRYM: Did he happen by chance to lose it?

LOKI: Not exactly to lose.

THRYM: Misplace? Then did he misplace—?

LOKI: No, someone possibly stole
The precious hammer of Thor,
The hammer he loves so dear.

THRYM: How dear?

LOKI: As dear as a casket of gold, perhaps,
A casket too heavy for ten
Of the strongest giants of Jotun
To carry up this hill.

THRYM: Dear Loki, kinsman, friend,
Let me, King Thrym, confide:
It was I and I alone
Who stole from under the nose
Of Thor, the God of War
The precious hammer which splits
The precious heads of the Jotuns
Morning, noon and night.
And now that hammer is hidden
Eight miles underground.
And for that hammer—

LOKI: You'll take—

THRYM: Not one casket of gold.
Not even ten, or a hundred.

LOKI: Then cows. A herd of cows,
A multitude, to feed
The Jotuns for ten years.

THRYM: Not even ten times more.

LOKI: Mares, to fill your stables.
The sleekest, swiftest mares—

THRYM: Freya.

LOKI: Freya!

THRYM: Freya.
Gorgeous, radiant Freya
To have for my ravishing bride.
For her alone did I steal

The deadly, magical hammer,
And for her alone will it be
Returned to that beast, God Thor.
LOKI: A hundred caskets of gold!
THRYM: Freya, only Freya.
LOKI: A thousand caskets, ten thousand!
THRYM: Freya, my idol, my love!
VOICE: Mad with a passion for Freya,
Thrym, great King of the Jotuns,
Is deaf to reason and sense.
A Jotun's lust for a goddess,
Loki tries to explain,
Is out of the question, can never
Be satisfied by the gods.
THRYM: No Freya, no hammer!
VOICE: Says Thrym,
And bids Loki farewell with a grin.
Loki leaves with foreboding,
Fainting at the thought
Of breaking the news to Freya,
Fearing for life and limb.

Scene 4

FREYA: Marry a Jotun! I!
VOICE: And her limpid, beautiful eyes
Weep their golden tears
As she lunges for hapless Loki,
But luckily Thor steps in.
THOR: No way,
VOICE: He says,
THOR: No way,
To keep our virgin Freya
From marrying that beast.
Refuse, and we lose dear Asgard,
Our heavenly, safe home.
Freya, decline these nuptials
And you send us to our doom.
VOICE: Hefty Freya leans
On the neck of the God of War
And drops more golden tears.
Staggering backward, Thor

Strokes her ample cheek
And soothes her with these words:
THOR: Seductive beauty, Freya,
    Victim of your own charms,
    Wed that beast, that Thrym,
    And all of us in heaven
    Will remember you forever,
    Honor you in absence,
    And applaud your sacrifice.
VOICE: She with a well-aimed blow
    Lays low the God of War.
FREYA: I in hell with Jotuns
    While the rest of you are lolling
    In the featherbed of heaven
    Swilling pots of mead?
    Never!
VOICE: And she lifts
    A threatening foot to crush
    The supine body of
    The terrified God of War.
    But Loki in compassion
    For his helpless, mighty lord,
    Leaps below the foot
    Of the bent-on-murder maid
    And with more than godly effort,
    Stays her lowering foot.
LOKI: Precious Freya, wait!
    Before you stomp and mangle
    The protector of the gods,
    Hear how cunning Loki
    Preserves you from this marriage
    And saves divinity!
VOICE: And suffering Freya, holding
    A ready foot above
    The bodies of the two,
    Looks down at both, and, glowering,
    Utters one word:
FREYA: Speak!
LOKI: One way, and only one!
    Thor himself must go
    To Thrym in Jotunheim

In Freya's wedding dress,
And play the blushing bride.
VOICE: In one bound, Thor is up
And on his feet, and lifts
A quaking Loki by
The throat, and shaking him,
Their noses touching, yells
Into his face:
THOR: WHAT!!
VOICE: But Freya, feeling salvation
Coming into view,
Tears Loki from the clutches
Of maddened, mighty Thor,
And presses him robustly
Against her grateful breast.
FREYA: The dear, the wily creature!
Oh, how the gods will thank him
For sparing me the insult
Of Jotun matrimony!
Virgin I am, and virgin
I'll innocently remain
Until a brave, a wise,
And lucky, lucky god
One day will win my hand.
Maiden Freya saved,
Thanks to the craft of Loki
And a bit of a ruse by Thor!
THOR: A bit of a ruse! By thunder,
How will it look for Thor
The manliest of the gods,
To dress in the virgin goddess
Freya's wedding dress?
FREYA: Lovely, it will look lovely!
And I'll give you the very sweetest,
Prettiest wedding dress,
And teach you the pretty ways
Of an innocent virgin maid.
VOICE: And she ran to her trousseau cupboard
And grabbed her wedding dress,
And slid it over the brawny frame
Of the warrior god of gods.

FREYA: Wonder of wonders, it fits
       As though it were made for him!
       A miracle that my dress
       Can encompass a bulk like his!
LOKI: The bulk, but not the beard,
      And the hair on his manly chest.
      We must cover his chest –
FREYA: With jewels,
       With my golden necklaces,
       And bracelets for his arms,
       And bangles for his ears.
LOKI: And what of the face?
FREYA: The face!
       We'll cover the face with a veil,
       A bridal veil, and a crown,
       A wedding crown for his head!
VOICE: And with all the garments and jewels
       Set on the god and in place,
       Loki and Freya step back,
       Observe, check, and appraise.
LOKI: Beautiful! Oh, dazzling!
      As dazzling as Freya herself!
      Now, walk!
VOICE: And raising a tree-stump leg,
       The god with effort waddles
       And trundles about the room.
FREYA: I? I walk like that?!
       NO, I will not be seen
       Tramping about like a clod!
       Grace, the grace of a goddess!
       Loki, my darling, show him
       The elegance of my walk!
VOICE: Loki, fearing the worst,
       Takes him by the hand
       And sashays and minces about
       With his partner, the God of War.
     Freya, in stupefied rage,
       Watches a moment or two,
       Then raises her arm to strike,
       To obliterate the sight
       Of the mockery of her grace

And her godly daintiness.
FREYA: Take off, take off my gown,
    My crown, my veil, my jewels!
    Freya will not be mocked
    By an oaf, a clod, a bear
    Who walks like an ape, not a woman,
    And shames the image of me.
VOICE: But Loki, not of a mind
    To note that the walk of Thor
    Is exactly like that of the goddess,
    Merely remarks to her:
LOKI: Freya, whatever his walk,
    Thor will have to make do.
VOICE: And Freya, weeping again
    Her stream of golden tears,
    Agrees that indeed, for the sake
    Of saving the realm of the gods,
    Indeed, it will have to do.
    She stifles her tears, and commands:
FREYA: Go, then! Go, and be wed,
    And try, oh try to be kind
    To the image of virgin and maid.
VOICE: But before he goes, the god,
    Feeling shamed as a man,
    Decides not to be shamed alone.
THOR: A bride unattended cannot
    Go to her wedding feast
    Without a retinue,
    Or even so much as a maid,
    And Loki, who thought of this ruse,
    Must certainly come as −
LOKI: NO!
VOICE: In a panic, he leaps for the door,
    But the mighty God of War
    Seizes him by the throat
    And calls to the goddess:
THOR: Freya!
    Dress him! Dress the maid!
VOICE: And Freya, delighted to have
    A maid with her at her feast,
    Grabs Loki and flies with him

To her trousseau cupboard once more.
LOKI: No! Oh, no! Oh, no!

Scene 5

VOICE: A burst of horns and trumpets,
>   And Loki, now gowned and aproned,
>   With borrowed tresses flowing
>   From under a modest cap,
>   And Thor, a massive poem
>   Of jewels and silks and veils,
>   Is greeted in the festive hall
>   Of the King of Jotuns, Thrym.
>   Seeing the wrapped-up maid
>   He imagines will be his bride,
>   He is overcome by the vision
>   Of her currently hidden charms,
>   And fainting with desire,
>   He beckons to bride and maid
>   To come at once to his table,
>   Then barks at his giant minions
>   To hurry up with the feast
>   And waste not a single moment
>   So that he and his bride may retire
>   And royally consummate.
> Hand in hand, the maid
>   And the stomping, clumping bride
>   Move slowly toward their places.
>   But watching his love, his goddess
>   Waddling toward her seat,
>   Thrym is taken aback,
>   And asks the mincing maid:
THRYM: Is this the gait of a goddess,
>   Waddling like a clod?
LOKI: It is, great King of Jotuns.
>   In Asgard, home of the gods,
>   All the goddesses waddle
>   As a mark of loveliness,
>   And of all of Asgard's goddesses,
>   Your bride waddles best.
THOR: Ah, then I will be
>   The proudest of all husbands,

For my bride waddles best!
Come, sit beside me, goddess!
VOICE: They sit, and Thor, on seeing
The table spread for feast,
Lifts his arm, and reaches
For the whole of a roasted steer.
The steer disappears in a flash
Under the bridal veil,
And soon as it's gone, Thor reaches
For two whole roasted pigs.
Thrym is aghast, and cries:
THRYM: Never in all my days
Did I see such a gluttonous bride!
LOKI: Small wonder, great king, the child
For eight long days has not eaten,
Wasting and pining for you.
VOICE: Thrym, overcome, cries out:
THRYM: Oh, let me kiss my bride!
The dear child, pining for me!
VOICE: And lifting the edge of her veil,
The lightning-beam of the eye
Of the bride of the king strikes fire,
And Thrym reels back, and cries:
THRYM: Why do her eyes glow red
Like the flames of a forest fire?
LOKI: Because the child hasn't slept
For eight long days, while waiting
And longing for her betrothed.
VOICE: Thrym is inflamed, and shouts
To his minions, the jotun giants:
THRYM: Hurry, and bring Thor's hammer
And lay it on Freya's lap,
And quick! Let's proceed at once
To sealing our marriage vows!
VOICE: He raises a beaker of mead
And cries for a wedding toast,
And Thor lifts a whole tun of mead
And pours it down at a gulp.
Thrym, in astonishment, gapes:
THRYM: Ah, my darling is parched,
Not having drunk a drop,

For eight days, yearning for me!

VOICE: The jotuns return with the hammer.
    Thrym grabs it, and gleefully
    Drops it into the lap
    Of his imminent bride-to-be.

THRYM: Now the bargain is sealed,
    And we, my love, will be joined
    Forever in perfect bliss!
    Bring the marriage ring!
    And darling, we'll make our vows!

THOR: Here is my vow!

VOICE: Bellows Thor,
    And pulling the veil from his face,
    Pitches the magic hammer
    Which magically flies through the air,
    Parting the heads of Thrym
    And the jotuns in one blow.
    As the hammer comes back to his hand,

THOR: Come on, little maid!

VOICE: He cries.
    And Loki, following, bleats:

LOKI: Oh, yes, dear bride,

VOICE: And they're gone.

Scene 6

VOICE: Now Thor, the God of War,
    With his wild red beard and his eye
    As bright and as fierce as fire,
    Chortles and laughs once more
    As he tosses his hammer in air,
    And again he hears the thud
    And after, the yell of pain,
    As the hammer finds in the hills
    Surrounding the heavenly home
    The heads of the jotun giants,
    For never again did a jotun
    Dare to steal the hammer
    Of Thor, the God of War,
    Whose breath rumbling like thunder,
    And his eye flashing like lightning,
    And his magic hammer daily

Splitting the skulls of the jotuns,
Kept forever the home of the gods
Safe from its enemies.

A Traveler's Unexpected Journal
Susana Montal

October 18th, 3:00 AM, Churchill, Canada

I peer through the darkness at those around me, thinking: How did I come to be here in this freezing gymnasium? We're in the arctic, in a snowstorm. It's the middle of polar bear season. Who are all these people snoring on their pallets a few feet away? I am waking up from a short nap, trying to orient myself to dreams or reality. I remember now. It was only a few days ago that I was strolling in the Louvre, meandering through the house of Madame de Sevigny, wandering about the dark and mysterious streets of Montmartre, and crossing the curved little bridge at Giverny across a pool of faded water lilies. But now, I am grateful to have these memories. Because I am still alive: shivering, exhausted, depending on the kindness of strangers. And outside, silent, watching, like prehistoric monoliths, are giant white polar bears casting their shadows across the snow-covered drifts.

October 17, 9:00 AM, Paris

I close my eyes and lean back into the soft upholstery of the Peugeot. The city falls away as we race towards the airport, taking back roads to escape the eternal traffic jams on the peripherique, the ring road which encircles Paris. I think of other places in the world I have experienced, places that still appear to me in dreams, each with their own intensity and meaning. The dreams create their own metaphors at each location. I believe, with St. Augustine, that "The world is a book, and those who do not travel read only a page."

October 17, 12:30 PM, Somewhere over the Atlantic

I look up from my in-flight magazine and study the positional graph—what a marvelous invention this is! How can I fear the massive, hurtling metal cylinder in which we sit, over which we as passengers have no control, when it is there up on the screen, like a charming toy that a child receives at Christmas. It reassures me... I love being able to see exactly where the plane is, precisely how many feet up in the air we are, how many hours we have flown and are yet to fly. It seems that all the routes from Los Angeles to Europe fly in an arc over Greenland. What could the reason for this be? Doesn't anyone fly directly from one point to another anymore? Perhaps it has to do with wanting to make us realize that it is very cold in other parts of the world, the revenge of an air traffic controller suffering through the winter somewhere in Michigan.

October 17, 2:14 PM, Somewhere off the Coast of Greenland

Water, water, and more water. The ocean beneath us—a piece of gleaming blue infinity. This blue I remember, from the house at Giverny, Monet's favorite place to work. The pond there was not this color, but exquisite in its serenity and finitude. Monet's love of the water is seen in all his works, from the paintings he did near the Seine to the Beach at Trouville. His depiction of the boardwalk as it narrows into the distance creates the perception of a long coastline. But here, I look out my window, touching the glass. Below me there is no opportunity for perspective— there is nothing but water, sky and not a single cloud.

October 17, 4:00 PM, Somewhere off the Coast of Greenland

My thoughts of the sea, the memories of Monet's waterscapes terminate abruptly as the flight crew rushes down the aisles at a dead heat towards the back of the plane. We all exchange frightened glances as the pilot then races back towards the cockpit. Was the cockpit door closed? Is someone else flying the plane now? Where are we going? And why? A train rushes through my mind bringing with it a journey through snow-covered mountains of the Black Forest. I'm waiting to disembark near a famous castle, struggling to understand the announcements of the train's conductor. Where will we be disembarking? I have no idea if I will miss my stop. I look around at the others, gripping the armrests. A feeling of helplessness like now, the train continuing on its way, the flight with a destination suddenly unknown and unforeseen to any of us.

October 17, 4:07 PM, Somewhere off the Coast of Greenland

We slow... and we drop. We are descending rapidly. I've forgotten how to breathe, and force myself to take in some air, in, out. We are still flying straight, dropping fast, slowing down suddenly. But there's no place to land. Voices rise around me, fearfully demanding explanations—the crew gives no information. Their faces tell us more than words can—we are in danger. Looking out the window on my left, I see plumes of liquid shooting out from the wing. So now we are jettisoning our fuel—I know this means we are lightening the plane for an emergency landing, but where? The last time I looked at the positional map, we were flying somewhere over the Atlantic—between Greenland and Canada. I watch my hands shaking as I take out the life jacket instructions—why hadn't I paid more attention before? I knew that my hands were looking for something, anything to do, to touch some cord, some sign, some button. Now, these hands, my hands, are holding other hands—will we kneel together, for a benediction, with whatever moments we have left? Every second is a blessing, a precious gift.

October 17, 4:40 PM, Somewhere over the Atlantic

We are flying much closer to the water. I can see the choppy water waiting below. How cold will it be? My hands fumble with my hair, to bind it up in case I find myself in that choppy water, swimming, helping others. I watch as my hands remove my earrings. But, really, why am I doing this? How long would we last in water that cold, assuming the plane did not break apart on impact? Too late for rational thinking about this—I decide to prepare for landing. Looking around quickly now, I try to see if there is anyone near me who might need help exiting the plane. I put on my gloves, reassuring some sitting close by who cannot see out of my window, that we must be preparing to land because we are dumping fuel from the wing. (Read as: hope!) But I see only fear in their eyes. I have never seen or felt fear like this around me. But I feel strangely calm, as though all my senses have been activated, filling me with a primordial instinct to survive at any cost. By now the pilot's voice is heard over the speakers—has it been half an hour or more since he ran up the aisle? He tells us that we have been cleared to make an emergency landing in Northern Canada.

October 17, 5:06 PM, Somewhere off the Coast of Canada

Watching, watching, taking another breath and still only blue… then, slowly, beautifully, tendrils of white snaking into the sea. Now a few evergreens are visible in the snow—we arc and approach a tiny lane in the middle of nothing—is it a road or a runway? As we touch snow and ground, the landing is breathtakingly smooth—I and everyone on the plane know that the danger is past. We look at each other in wonder and relief, hardly believing our luck! I want to get off the plane immediately and feel the earth under me. To pick up a handful of snow and watch it sift through my fingers to the ground below.

October 17, 5:15 PM, Churchill, Canada

We applaud, we celebrate our arrival! All of us are speaking at once, aware that we are so lucky. Munching on brie and butter sandwiches, we relax and wait till they find a way to get us all off the plane. Outside my window I see a fire truck with a small platform trying to maneuver up to the emergency exit door. The stewardesses are smiling, excited, overwhelmed like the rest of us. Those of us who can, translate the pilot's announcements for the German and Spanish speakers on board. But several hours later, euphoria is replaced by exhaustion and frustration—we can't leave the plane for at least six hours. When a plane lands unexpectedly in this new time of terrorist threats, much red tape must be cleared before anyone can disembark. Meanwhile, the local emergency response team organizes to meet our arrival with transportation, food and shelter at the closest town: Churchill, population 1,000. We are here, in the arctic region, where the northern lights are visible, in the middle of polar bear season. After eight hours, the emergency chutes are inflated and we slide down them into the snow. I forget to put my knees up and come down too fast. I look up as I rocket down the chute, the people below looking anxious and positioning themselves to soften my landing. But I hit the ground safely and quickly stand up to show I'm alright. As we wrap ourselves in thick woolen blankets, we see the busses waiting for us. They are from the local tour company that takes tourists to see the polar bears nearby. Another passenger and I ask our tour driver to take us out to see the bears now. But he assures us he will drive us out later, after we have rested and had dinner. He rushes over to tell a desperate smoker to put out her cigarette, that there's no smoking on the tarmac. But she refuses. After all, she insists, she has been on the plane for over twelve hours!

October 18, 12:33 AM, Churchill, Canada

The conditions of travel have changed dramatically. Travel is no longer imposed by exile, or great need. Oedipus was forced to take his journey alone, to wander as a stranger, with no family or friends, save Antigone, for the rest of his life, scorned and mistreated, left to beg for the mercy of hostile strangers. But there are no hostile strangers here. First-World travelers who have met with misfortune now have no need to beg. Those of us stranded here are offered food, hot drinks, hastily assembled blankets and mattresses, whatever can be found to comfort and sustain us in our predicament. There is nothing to do but wait for another eight hours till a rescue plane can be found, equipped with a retractable stairway, and the capability to fly in arctic conditions. We are told that these are not as readily available as other aircraft. I wonder what it will be like? I've flown through major snowstorms before, and I remember how frightening they can be. Circling over an airport in Kansas City for a long time, going up, then down, again and again, with no visibility. The captain would not explain why we were so close to the airport and could not land. The bar service was working overtime to calm the passengers.

October 18, 3:47 AM, Churchill, Canada

During the night's long wait, I rest briefly on the gymnasium floor, covering my head, cocooning, with a blanket to protect myself. It is very cold. Mattresses are laid out everywhere, a mosaic of old quilts and blankets. A chorus of snores resounds in the large space, somehow comforting. After several hours, one plane takes half of us away. Six hours later, that same plane will return to shuttle the rest of us to the comfort of a hotel in Winnipeg, another two hours flight away. I sleep and dream again. In this dream I am on another plane, circling the earth again and again. I try to look out the window, but I can see nothing. Inside the plane it is snowing. Suddenly I awake with a start, but only because someone snored very loudly on the mattress next to me. I listen to his snores and realize I will not be able to sleep any more.

October 18, 4:00 AM, Churchill, Canada

In darkness we make our way through the arctic tundra, towards the landing strip outside of Churchill. It is 4:00 AM, and I am disappointed. I still haven't seen a polar bear. I watch intently as we drive through white blankets of freshly fallen snow. I see a big lump out there in the drifts. I rub the icy bus window with the back of my sleeve, and there, for a moment, I look out at something huge and white with dark hollows around its eyes.

October 18, 8:36 AM, Winnipeg, Canada

At last the opportunity to lie, at the limits of exhaustion, in a soft bed at the hotel. There's only three hours to sleep before the flight to Los Angeles. I think again of all the people who have helped us, beginning with the emergency rescue team, and of their long, sleepless night following our arrival. They worked through their exhaustion to help us off the plane and protect us from the harshness of the climate there. They prepared our dinner and found mattresses for us to rest upon after our ordeal. They took some of us out on tour buses in the early morning hours, in the hopes of seeing more of the bears roaming in the darkness, looking for food. I must sleep, I force myself to rest. As my head touches the pillow, I am lost in a dream. I am diving into a pool of water, soundless, dark and blue. Swimming deeper and deeper, I wonder how much longer I can hold my breath. But I have no need for air. Through the depths I see something far away, luminescent and beckoning. I try to reach it, but it falls further into a blue abyss. At last I reach it, grasp it in my hand. Heavier now, I pull myself up through the water. I reach the surface and open my hand to see what I'm holding. A pearl. The alarm wakes me. I walk without fear to my next flight—waiting on the runway for me.

My Mother and the Virgin Mary
Barbara Ponse

Pamela picked up the box of chocolates from the seat, stepped out of the rental car, locked the door, and walked to the glass entryway. She stopped, peered through the window, sucked in her breath, her hand at her throat. Her mother, standing at the other side of the glass, made the same gesture. Pamela stepped back. "Mother!" Mouthing the word "mother," the figure in the glass retreated, hand at her throat. Pamela was looking at her own reflection.

She pushed the red release button. The doors swung open. She tiptoed through the room, avoiding the eyes of the old women. Like withered doves, they perched in their wheelchairs. One time a woman had called out to her, "are you coming to take me home?" Pamela had run this gauntlet before.

She came to the hallway that led to her mother's ward. She held her breath, trying not to breathe the urine smell. A blond woman, younger-looking than the other residents, blocked the way with her wheelchair. Her eyes shone bright with terror as she whistled and flapped her hands as though they were on fire. Pamela slid past her, threaded her way through the crones lining the hallway, heard someone moan from an open doorway.

The pink-faced woman at the reception desk smiled at her when Pamela asked for her mother. "I'm here to see Gertrude Rose. I'm her daughter, Pamela, from California."

"Just a sec, Hon, I'll see if we can find her for ya!" She craned her neck over the counter and called down the hall to an Asian woman. "Betsy! Is Gert in the Sunshine Room? Her daughter's here, from *Californya!*" The woman's flat nasal speech sounded just like the way her family spoke, except for herself and her mother. She suppressed a smile. California was still exotic in the small town where her mother's nursing home sat squat and brown near the Connecticut River.

Betsy came to the front desk. "She's sitting in there." Betsy touched Pamela's arm then pointed down the hall. "Come, I'll take you to her."

Standing side by side, Betsy barely reached Pamela's shoulder. "Have you been here before?" They started to walk down the long yellow corridor.

"Yes. But I live so far away, it's hard to get here as much as I'd like. How is my mother doing?"

"Her feet bother her. The podiatrist took off some of the bigger calluses. But it's hard to get her to soak her feet. You know, Gert won't do anything she doesn't want to!" She leaned toward Pamela and lowered her voice. "She's so stubborn! She treats everyone like they're her children, you know, patients, staff, everybody! We've taken to feeding her last. Otherwise, she'll give away her food, always worried that somebody's hungry!"

Pamela stopped short, Betsy stopped too.

"My mother's feet were run over by a trolley when she was a little girl." The words rushed out. Pamela looked down at the box of chocolates. Her hands trembled.

"Oh my! Run over! How terrible!" Betsy looked up at Pamela. "Oh I'm so sorry. The poor thing!"

Pamela continued looking down. It had been years since she'd first heard about the trolley running over her feet. She remembered how shocked she was that Gertrude had never told her own mother, Pamela's grandmother, about the accident.

"Why? Why didn't you tell Grandma?"

"It would have made her angry. She would have blamed me."

"But why? It wasn't your fault! Why would she blame you?"

"Oh, she would have, she would have! That's all."

Betsy and Pamela walked slowly towards the Sunshine Room.

Ever since she was a child, Pamela had worried about her mother. She used to be her mother's shadow, following her around the house. Her mother walked with her head thrust forward, her back inclined, wincing as she took a step. She saw pain in her mother's face, watched her lips move, heard her muttering in a whispery voice.

"Mama, what are you saying?"

"Oh I'm... I'm praying, dear."

"Are you praying for me?"

"For everybody, dear. I'm praying for everybody."

Betsy interrupted Pamela's reverie. She looked up and tried to reassure her.

"You know, dear, her feet... nothing stops your mother from getting around. In fact, she's always walking, up and back, up and back, patrolling the halls! She moves so much, we have to make sure she eats enough so she doesn't lose too much weight! She has her own little route, checking laundry bins, rewashing dishes, making beds! Sometimes she'll remake a bed even when we're trying to put somebody in it! But her favorite thing is pushing the other patients in their wheelchairs! She'll give them a ride, whether they like it or not." Betsy laughed, put her hand on Pamela's arm, and pushed her gently forward.

Light poured from the doorway to the Sunshine Room. Pamela stopped and turned to face Betsy, her back to the open doorway. She looked into Betsy's kind, brown face and attempted a smile. She forced her voice to be cheerful. "Oh, I know! The last time I was here, my mother commandeered a woman's wheelchair! The woman was wheeling down the corridor on her own when my mother took charge. She grabbed the chair. The poor woman began to howl, but my mother was determined. She seized the handle on one side of the chair. The woman tried to get away; she sped up. Undaunted, my mother swung her body and the chair like a wrangler. She captured the other handle and rode that chair like a bronco 'til she hit the wall, her captive wailing all the way! By the way, did she get the baby carriage and the dolls I sent her?"

Betsy neared the entrance to the room, Pamela a step behind her. "Oh, was that you that sent that beautiful carriage?" She glanced over her shoulder.

"Yeah, she's always looking for her babies, I thought she might enjoy it."

"It's in her room, by her bed. She likes the dolls sometimes. But she likes the live ones best!" Betsy stopped and gazed at Pamela, her head cocked slightly to the side as if she were waiting for something. They were standing together in the doorway. Pamela's mother sat across the room. Pamela felt frozen to the spot. Then Betsy made a move toward Gertrude; Pamela followed close behind her. "Gert! Someone's here to see you! From California! Now Gert, you be a good girl! She's come a long way to see you!" Betsy spoke to Pamela's mother as if she were a naughty child. She pushed Pamela forward, murmured

"Have a nice visit!" and left the room.

Pamela gazed at her mother slumped in the faded tapestry armchair. She shook her head. Her mother's eyes looked dark and empty; her glasses were gone. The last time Pamela had come to visit, her mother had called her an impostor, someone pretending to be her daughter.

"You must have a mother somewhere," Gertrude had said, "but it's not me!" Now she seemed not to notice that anyone was there at all.

Gertrude's white hair stuck out in tufts on one side of her head; eczema crusted at her hairline. Pamela closed her eyes and bent down to kiss her mother on the cheek. Her mother's breath assailed her, and seeing the stains on the bodice of her flowered housedress, and her mother's feet, purple with veins, swelling over the tops of her slippers made her almost cry out loud.

"If this happens to me, I hope someone shoots me!" Pamela said to herself. She held her breath, kissed her mother cheek again, and made little smacking sounds with her lips. Sometimes she could make her mother laugh. Now, Gertrude just gave a small sigh.

"Mother, it's me, Pamela!" She gazed into her mother's eyes. They appeared bottomless, like the forbidden quarry hole where Pamela secretly swam as a child. She realized that she'd dreamt about the quarry hole the night before. She stood on a boulder on the quarry shore and dove into the green black water. The water grew icy as she descended. She could hear her mother's warning in her ears. "Don't you go swimming in that quarry hole! It has no bottom!" In the dream, Pamela felt a pull on her body. Something sucked her deeper; something was sucking her down to China! She flailed to the surface and cried out to the receding shore. She awoke with a start.

Pamela put her hand on her mother's arm and caressed her. The flesh on her mother's jowls trembled as she opened her mouth to speak.

"Tik, tik, tik, tik, tik!" She sputtered. "Tik, tik, tik, tik!"

Gertrude's use of language had once been beautiful and precise. As her mind lost its bearings, she'd slipped from repeated questions to fractured phrases, then to disjointed words, and now to sounds. The ticking was new.

Pamela turned away, swallowing hard. She recalled the first

time she had come here to visit her mother. Her niece, Marie, and Marie's baby daughter, Alicia, had come with her. They'd found Gertrude sitting in a geri chair in the rec room, staring into space. A dozen or so old women in wheelchairs or geri chairs were lined up against the walls.

"Mother! Look who's here to see you! Marie and her new baby girl, Alicia! Your *great*-grand daughter! You're a *great* grandma!" Pamela greeted her mother with a kiss.

"Thank you, sweetheart, thank you!" Gertrude shivered and kissed Pamela's hands.

"Here, Grandma! Hold the baby, Grandma! Hold, Alicia!" Marie put her baby in Gertrude's arms.

Though Gertrude recognized Pamela, she had no idea who Marie was. Despite repeated explanations, she continually mistook Alicia for a little boy. Marie, who had not seen her grandmother for many months, was devastated to see how deteriorated she'd become. She signaled Pamela that she would wait for her in the car.

Gertrude, indifferent to Marie's leaving, continued to coo at the baby in her arms. "You little dickens, be a good boy now!"

The falsetto whine of "The Duke of Earl" sounded from the loudspeakers overhead. An energetic woman in a blue sweat suit appeared in front of the denizens lined up against the wall. Her spiked red hair, like a corona, bobbed in rhythm while she worked her arms and exhorted the old women. Pamela took the baby from her mother and started to dance. Gertrude plucked at the corner of her chair while the wizened souls began to wave their arms to the music.

"Come on girls! One-two! One-two! Move those arms, girls! Feel the beat! One-two! One-two!" cried the redhead.

"Duke, Duke, Duke, Duke of Earl, Duke, Duke, Duke of Earl, Duke, Duke." The music thudded on. Pamela danced, her tears falling on the baby she held in her arms.

An attendant approached her mother's chair and started to push her toward the door.

"Wait! Wait! I'm her daughter," Pamela called out. The attendant would not be deterred. "Your mother needs to take her meds now."

"Mom!"

Her mother turned her head and looked at her.

"I love you, Mom!"

"I love you too, sweetheart." The attendant wheeled her out of the room.

That was the last time her mother had known who she was. Now, Pamela listened to her mother tick. She remembered the chocolates she'd brought. "Mother! Chocolates! Your favorite!" Pamela almost shouted. Gertrude stopped ticking. Pamela opened the chocolates, spread the paper cover, and proffered the candy. "C'mon sweetheart! Look, Mom, mmm! Chocolates! Try one! They're good!"

Her hand trembling, Gertrude reached for the chocolate. Her blunt fingers slipped over the smooth surfaces. She grabbed a piece, with its paper cup, and put both in her mouth. "No, Mama! No, no! We don't eat paper!" Gertrude, chocolate and paper protruding from her lips, began to laugh. Pamela grinned at her and retrieved the paper.

"S'good! S'good!"

"Take another one! Would you like another one? Just chocolate, no paper!" She crouched in front of her mother. Gertrude took another piece and popped it into her mouth. She sat absorbed, chewing. Pamela began pacing back and forth; images and memories jumbled in her mind. She watched herself moving, seemingly without will, toward the door. Aware of her mother's voice, her urgent tone, she turned and moved back to her.

"My father, my father, is he home yet?" Her mother's eyes widened with fear.

"No, mother, not yet. He won't be here for a while."

Pamela tried to follow her mother's lead. She knew only fragments of her mother's history. She knew that her mother was four years old when her father fell off a train and was killed. She knew her grandmother had then married a drunkard. "House-devil street-angel, he was!" her mother used to say. This was the "father" her mother meant: her stepfather. He'd been long dead but lived on still in her fractured memory.

"PamDickSal…" her mother began, merging her children's names together, as indeed she'd done most of their lives.

"They're fine, mother. They're not home from school yet. It's early."

Gertrude seemed reassured, but only for a moment. She began ticking again, louder than before. "Tik, tik, tik, tik, tik,

tik!" she sputtered like an engine trying to start. "Tik, tik, tik, tik, tik!" She sounded furious now, determined.

Pamela tried to soothe her, to break through the chanting. She spoke softly, caressed her worn arms, but to no avail. The ticking sped up and became louder. Her mother, the mother she knew, was lost in her own world.

Pamela waited for the ticking storm to pass. The thought pressed in on her that death would be better than this fear-filled, mindless life. She recalled that her mother used to say that, when she died, she hoped she would be worthy of a beatific vision. A holy preview of the life-to-come at the moment of death would give meaning and purpose to her life on earth. At the time, Pamela had recoiled at the idea of a life lived for a vision at the moment of death. Now, she found herself praying that her mother could have her wish fulfilled.

"Tik, tik, tik!" Gertrude's accelerated ticking broke into Pamela's thoughts. Suddenly, she had a wild image of what her mother was attempting to do. She was revving her motor! She was trying to fly! "Go! Mother! Go!" She cheered as Gertrude gunned the engine faster and faster. The chair beneath her shook and creaked with the strain. Faster! faster! "Tik, tik, tik!" The blades whined and crashed like cymbals as they spun. She was ready for take-off!

"Mother!" Pamela cried, moved and proud. Her mother left the chair and soared skyward. Up she went, her housedress flapping against her legs as she rose into the air. "Mother! Watch your head!" Pamela warned, fearing her mother would hit the ceiling. But the ceiling evaporated as if in anticipation of her ascent.

Light suffused the air. From the corner of heaven, Pamela saw the Virgin Mary waft down to greet her mother as she sailed upward. The Virgin's blue gown furled and unfurled as she drifted. Her veil, like incandescent wings, spread across the violet sky. Her mother and the Virgin stood together in the air above her head.

"Gert," said Mary warmly, her hands outstretched. "You finally made it! I've been watching over you!" The Virgin touched the silvery down on Gertrude's face. Her holy laughter tinkled through the air.

Pamela saw that her mother's humble housedress had been transformed into a white satin robe; the stains on her bodice, bursts of roses. She saw her mother smile shyly at the Virgin Mother. She'd stopped ticking. Earthly trouble had no hold on her now. Faith and grace kept her aloft. The Virgin's eyes shone like two crescent moons as she waited for Gertrude to speak.

"I... I tried to be good. I really did try!" Gertrude spoke with the soft brogue of her own mother. "Sometimes it wasn't easy!"

The Virgin's laugh burbled through the sky. "Of course! Of course you did! But that's all over now!"

"What can she mean? What is all over now?" Pamela wondered. "Is my mother dying? Is this her Beatific Vision?" She called out to the Virgin, "Heavenly Mother! My mother was very good! She suffered all her life for the Life Hereafter! All her life!"

The Blessed Virgin turned her holy face toward Pamela. Her eyes were stern. "Aren't you the one who caused all the trouble? Aren't you the one who forsook my BELOVED SON? MY ONLY BEGOTTEN SON WHO DIED ON THE CROSS FOR YOUR SINS? THE DEVIL TAKE YOU!" Her curse blasted through the ether.

All her young life, Pamela's father had admonished her: "Model yourself after the Virgin Mary and your mother!" Pamela knew even then that she couldn't be like either of them: worse, knew she didn't want to be. Her failure was now enunciated throughout the universe.

"I tried to tell her," her mother pled with the Virgin. "But she was always too much for me! Smart, too smart for her own good!"

Pamela fell to her knees. "Please!" she cried out to the Virgin. "My mother did try! She said God wanted me to be a Carmelite nun and do penance for the sins of the world. It was I who couldn't do it! I couldn't do God's will. She taught me all my prayers! The Confiteor, the Apostles' Creed, I can still say the Lord's Prayer in Latin!" As if her pitiful recital would mean anything now! "But I could not believe! I had to follow my conscience! I don't believe in the Devil!" She beseeched the Virgin, "It's not my mother's fault!"

The Virgin glowered at her, "WHAT YOU BELIEVE AND DON'T BELIEVE MATTERS NOT! BLESSED IS SHE WHO DOES NOT UNDERSTAND AND YET BELIEVES. YOU AND YOUR PRIDE! YOUR INTELLIGENCE!" she spat out the words. "SO YOU DON'T BELIEVE IN THE DEVIL? WELL, THE DEVIL BELIEVES IN YOU!"

The virgin's voice pierced the blackened sky. Clouds guttered like flames over the horizon. The Virgin's eyes, no longer moons, glittered. The gleam of blood shone on her black lips.

Lucifer! Masquerading as the Virgin! The Devil takes a thousand shapes, her mother had warned. The Brightest Angel can possess you even against your will! The Devil/Virgin's mouth twisted in a terrible grimace. Infernal cries filled the air.

"Don't, don't, please don't hurt my mother!" Pamela sprang to her feet, spread out her arms, clenched her muscles till her veins were ropes in her arms. Stood on Golgotha while the Devil rained hatred on her head.

When she was a child, her mother had told her the only way to ward off the Devil was to say the Sacred Name of Jesus a thousand times. Now, in a fever, she repeated His Holy Name. Her head bobbed up and down with each pious ejaculation. Taut and drenched, the blood flowed from her brow and reddened her tears.

The sound of beating wings filled the air. Pamela looked heavenward, saw her mother fly at the Virgin and clutch her fast. Together they soared higher and higher until they became a single spark at the apex of the world. Then they disappeared. Pamela shivered and fell forward, her face in her mother's lap. She heard her mother whisper: "If you save one life, you save the whole world!"

"Oh I tried to save you, Momma. I couldn't! I couldn't save the one life I wanted to save!" Pamela mourned. Like music, like a blessing her mother's words poured over her. "You don't understand. The life you save must be your own!"

Pamela looked up into her mother's bottomless eyes. The light she'd thought she'd seen was extinguished, but the words she'd heard stayed with her. She took her mother's hands in her own and kissed them, then rose to her feet. She gazed at her mother, her heart heavy with love, and bent down to kiss her cheek once more before she left.

The Scissors
James Ragan

The librarian cracks the book's spine twice,
precisely, punishing the paper with her thumb,
as if each page might leap loose of the rib's stitching
to gauze the eyes in swaths of skin
or mute the mouth with the word rush of meaning,
fierce and feral as a fever itching.

The scissors she has cradled, twin-lobed,
in the sheath of an apron finds her fingers, stained
with the hieroglyphics of ink she might devour
like a prune sauce or cloth that still needs paring.
She has trained in the language of its cut
and just as clean the stripping down of fact to glue.

She has learned to wedge the title first
between each blade and in a quick slice,
sheer the offending allusion, much too rich
in opinion, a guilty verse, each syllable
to her weaver's grasp, lost, and just as swiftly
a page shorn from the content's mast.
Here is the future mending the carpet of its past.

High Notes
Tyler Craft Cormney

Author's Note:

Tony Pagliacci, a rootless countertenor, might seem an unlikely hero. In the original comedy High Notes*, this struggling American opera singer travels to Italy to reconnect with his roots and to find the poetry that is missing in his day-to-day life.*

In the opening scene, we find our nostalgic icon in the throes of a passionate daydream. Throughout the film, we travel between dream and reality, past and present; sometimes it is difficult to tell which is which:

The score for the aria *"Vesti La Giubba"* from Leoncavallo's opera I PAGLIACCI begins over BLACK.

FADE IN:

INT. LA SCALA OPERA HOUSE - MILAN, ITALY - NIGHT

We travel through the auditorium of the most famous opera house in all the world: ornate white ceilings, sculptures, the plaster masks of Comedy and Tragedy.

THE AUDITORIUM

is filled to capacity with finely dressed ITALIAN PATRONS, their faces eager with anticipation.

CENTER STAGE

A light comes up on the clown, PAGLIACCIO, separating him from matted darkness. He looks up. His eyes sparkle with tears as he begins Canio's famous lament, *"Vesti la Giubba"* --

>   PAGLIACCIO (THE CLOWN)
>   *"Recitar! Mentre presso dal delirio..."*

The singer has an unusually high tenor voice. Technically, he's a countertenor, and the Aria was composed for a standard tenor, so we are witnessing a singular performance. PAGLIACCIO'S song continues to the final stanza:

>   PAGLIACCIO (THE CLOWN)
>   *"...Tramuta in lazzi lo spasmo ed il pianto; in una smorfia il singhiozzo e'l dolor. Oh ridi, Pagliaccio, sul tuo amore in franto!"*

Tears stream down his cheeks. He drops to one knee and opens his arms to the heavens:

>   PAGLIACCIO (cont'd)
>   (singing the finale)
>   *"Ridi del duol t'avvelena il cor!"*

Pagliaccio bows his head.

We hear the THUNDERING APPLAUSE of the opera house.

Suddenly, and all at once, the round of applause ends.

Silence.

The Clown looks up. In a flash, his fantasy world disintegrates:

We hear the clink of silverware, muffled chatter, bawdy laughter.

THE CLOWN'S POV - LA SCALA OPERA HOUSE

is now a dingy dinner theater. The enthralled OPERA FANS have been replaced by indifferent DINERS, stuffing their faces, slurping their wine, cracking their ribald jokes.

COSTUMED WAITERS weave among the tables pouring cheap chianti: AN ENGLISH DANDY, A VIKING PRINCESS, A GYPSY GIRL CHOMPING A CIGAR.

THE CLOWN looks down at his own costume. It is now an ill-fitting moth-eaten, button-missing replica of the ornate costume from his fantasy. The sadness in the Clown's eyes is heartbreaking, but this is no longer an act. His head hangs low as he starts off stage. Then --

A well-dressed ITALIAN GENTLEMAN at a table near the stage begins to clap for him. He's the only one. In fact, he stands up from his table while applauding.

The Clown pauses and smiles, tipping his bowler hat.

The Curtain falls. Its surface proudly proclaiming:

"LA SCALA RISTORANTE, NEW YORK
Home of the Singing Waiter"

INT. THE WINGS - SAME

A step off stage, the Clown's smile
vanishes and his shoulders slump. He
passes the next dreamer waiting for her
cue, a rotund VIKING PRINCESS. To her
he doesn't exist -- there are no Italian
clowns in her opera.

*When he learns that his biological mother is dying, Tony travels
to the fictional city of Santa Cecilia, Italy, to say farewell. This will be
their first meeting since she gave him up for adoption twenty years
ago. He has so many questions, but she is too weak to speak anything
more than the name she gave him. For now, his questions must remain
unanswered.*

*Like a detective, Tony searches Santa Cecilia for clues that will
give him some indication of who his mother was, and, perhaps, who
he is in the process. Leonardo Mazza, who becomes Tony's guide and
confidant, tells him that "the very soul of Santa Cecilia is music... At
least it used to be."*

*The city of Santa Cecilia is tottering on the brink of the twenty-
first century. The standards of its golden era are rapidly disappearing.
As another character puts it, "It used to be in Italy there were two
powers you did not cross—God and Opera." But times have appar-
ently changed: Santa Cecilia's Opera House has been condemned and
is scheduled to be demolished. In Violetta's words from the opera* La
Traviata, *it is time to say* "addio, del passato bei sogni ridenti"—
"farewell past, happy dreams of days gone by."

*Tony learns that his mother was once an opera singer, who
couldn't make ends meet. Even after giving him up for adoption, she
was forced to leave the stage to earn a living wage. Through determina-
tion, she built a costume shop that served the local opera house. If she
couldn't be on the stage, at least her beautiful creations would be. Now,
with the opera house closed, her legacy is in jeopardy.*

*Tony visits the costume shop, which was left to him in his mother's
will. Inside he meets ghosts of the past, clowns of the present, and a
vision of the future:*

INT. COSTUME SHOP - NIGHT

Tony enters. The shop is dimly lit and

deserted.

THE COSTUMES

look like a royal court of headless
ghosts.

MUSIC is playing softly from the back of
the shop.

Tony listens at the door of his mother's
office. The music is coming from inside. He
opens the door.

INT. THE OFFICE - SAME

The song is "*Un Aura Amorosa*" from
Mozart's *Cosi Fan Tutte*.

When Tony enters, he sees --

A MAN'S ARMS hugging the waist of a DRESS
DUMMY.

> TONY
> Excuse me.

Rodolfo, the street singer, releases the
dress dummy and jumps back.

> RODOLFO
> (blushing)
> *Mi scusi! Mi scusi!*

> TONY
> What are you doing?

Rodolfo, tipping his top hat repeatedly --

> RODOLFO
> *Buona notte! Buona notte!*

Quack quack!

He runs out past Tony. Tony shakes his head. He stops the record player. The music stops.

                                    DISSOLVE TO:

INT. THE OFFICE - A FEW MINUTES LATER

A lonely cot in the corner and a rack of women's clothes.

BLACK AND WHITE PHOTOS

of his mother with various opera stars on the wall.

Tony pulls a framed photo from the wall.

THE PHOTO

is of his mother, twenty years ago. She's standing next to a young LUIGI CANTINORI in his Pagliacci costume.

                    TONY (V.O.)
          Cantinori...

                                    CUT TO:

A BABY ALBUM

Pictures of Tony as an infant. He stops on --

A PHOTOGRAPH

Tony, age three, facing his mother, who is the same age as she was in the photo with Cantinori. She's dressed in the white gown she was wearing in Tony's nightmare on the plane. Her hands cup his tiny face.

Tony touches his tingling cheeks as if remembering.

BABY ALBUM

After this page, the rest are blank.

Tony opens the blinds of a window facing the shop floor.

THE SHOP FLOOR

The costumes look so empty without bodies inside them.

Tony's eyes reveal the loneliness in his heart. He turns away from the window and notices something that he wasn't conscious of before --

THE DRESS DUMMY

that Rodolfo was hugging is draped in a WHITE GYPSY GOWN, the same dress seen in the album photo and in Tony's nightmare.

Tony closes the office blinds.

ANOTHER ANGLE - THE RECORD PLAYER

Tony lowers the needle. The music begins again, "Un Aura Amorosa."

ANOTHER ANGLE - TONY AND THE DRESS DUMMY

He carefully wraps his arms around the dress dummy and sways gently with the music.

Moments later, a woman's voice interrupts him:

                    WOMAN'S VOICE (O.S.)
          Mi scusi.

Tony, still holding the dress dummy, spins
around, half-expecting to see his mother's
ghost.

ANGELINA BIRENZE

is about his age. Her devastating beauty
is accentuated by the vulnerability of a
lost child.

                    ANGELINA
               (in Italian, subtitled)
          <Is the Signorina in?>

Tony steps around the dress dummy.

                    TONY
          She's...No.   Can   I   help
          you?

                    ANGELINA
          Mi dispiace. English. Am I
          late?

Her English is very good.

                    TONY
          For what?

                    ANGELINA
          My lesson.

                    TONY
          Sorry...?

Pause.

                    ANGELINA
          Just tell her that I stopped
          by.

She starts to go.

                    TONY
          What's your name?

                    ANGELINA
                (laughing nervously)
          Oh. Angelina Birenze.

Angelina turns, intent on leaving.

                    TONY
          Signorina Birenze, wait.

Angelina turns back to face him.

                    TONY (cont'd)
          I'm sorry to be the one
          to tell you...Signorina
          Cassini has passed away.

Angelina clutches her heart.

                    ANGELINA
          Oh...Oh no!

                    TONY
          You...studied with her?

                    ANGELINA
          Not...no. I met her on a
          train at the beginning of
          the summer. I've been away.
          I've just -- she told me to
          come when I -- *Ah Dio*. Poor
          woman.

She crosses herself.

                    TONY
          She was my mother.

Angelina bursts into tears.

                    ANGELINA
          I feel...I -- *dispiace.*

Angelina runs out of the office. Tony
chases after her --

                    TONY
          Signorina!

    Tony embarks on a quest through the past for beauty. He finds it represented in the condemned Opera House, in the costume shop that his mother built with her own hands, and in the person of Angelina Birenze, a vulnerable, young Italian woman who is searching for her own share of beauty and independence. High Notes *is a film about searching our past for answers.*

    Tony falls in love with Angelina, but she is engaged to Enzo Stavione, the most powerful man in Santa Cecilia. Enzo also happens to be the real estate developer responsible for closing the opera house and trying to put Tony's mother's costume shop out of business. When Tony stands up to Enzo, his life is endangered. In order to stay in Santa Cecilia, he must disguise himself as a female singing tutor named Mona Lisa.

EXT. UNIVERSITY CAMPUS - SANTA CECILIA -
DAY

The love duet from Puccini's Madame
Butterfly --

"Vogliatemi bene" -- plays over.

Mona Lisa makes her debut on campus. It's
a magical day when anything seems possible
--

A violet sky, majestic poplar trees, a
monarch butterfly.

Mona Lisa's long, yellow scarf flutters in
the wind.

"She" sees a group of six YOUNG WOMEN
sitting on a picnic blanket having tea.

THE TEA PARTY

In Tony's mind's eye, the tea party
becomes a Picasso painting -- a cubist
tea party: glimpses of pastel colored
sundresses. A tea cup of bone china. A
woman's eye. A steaming tea pot. Pink
lips. Sun reflected off long hair. A
delicate hand. A plate of sweets. The
silhouette of a woman's neck and shoulder.

Then in the next moment, disparate images
combine into a unity of beauty -- Angelina
Birenze.

Angelina notices Mona Lisa staring at
her. She stands up from the tea party and
crosses to her.

Mona Lisa smiles at Angelina, and Angelina
returns the smile.

*Tony eventually learns that he must drop his mask if he is ever
going to find true love. When Angelina learns that she has been de-
ceived, she is understandably furious. Nevertheless, she recognizes that
his motives were pure. In true operatic fashion, she lets him know that
he is forgiven by singing a love duet that he composed for her. The
aria is written with male and female parts interchanging but never
overlapping—that is, until the end. High Notes ends like the aria, in
harmony:*

EXT. THE PARK - DUSK

A light snow is falling.

A haggard, bearded, half-dead Tony Pagliacci sings for loose change and huddles for body warmth.

On the wind, Tony thinks he hears a --

WOMAN SINGING.

He's delirious -- It may be his imagination.

                    TONY
          Papa did you hear...Papa?

Tony looks around, but he's alone.

He hears the song again and stumbles in the direction of the woman's voice.

EXT. STREETS OF SANTA CECILIA - SAME

He searches the winding streets. Suddenly, he's aware that this is the female part of Angelina's aria.

Tony struggles to sing the reply but can't; his voice has deserted him.

The Woman's voice leads him to --

INT. THE OPERA HOUSE - SAME

A light comes up on stage and we see a WOMAN'S SILHOUETTE behind the scrim.

Tony, exhausted and dressed in rags, climbs onto the stage and stands on the other side of the scrim.

He touches the silhouette lightly with his hand, certain it must be a mirage.

The woman sings softly.

Tony falls to his knees, removes his hat, and holds it out to her. Angelina's singing the final stanza of the aria he wrote for her -- THE HARMONY.

LEO, ESTELLA, RODOLFO, AND OTHERS

slip into the House quietly, unnoticed by Tony.

TONY

unties the moth-eaten scarf wrapped around his throat.

With all he has left, he attempts to join her song.

HIS VOICE

is brittle at first but slowly regains its former power.

THE SCRIM rises revealing --

ANGELINA

breathtaking in Tony's mother's white gypsy gown, the one that Rodolfo rescued from the fire.

HIS TIRED EYES

ignite with a new spark. Tony moves closer to her. She takes his free hand --

Their voices soar together. The song concludes.

Angelina holds his face in her hands, the same way that Tony's mother did in the old photograph.

APPLAUSE rises from the House.

Angelina looks into the audience and sees --

HER FATHER

shaking his fist above his head in emphatic celebration.

Angelina takes a bow.

LEO AND ESTELLA

smile at one another. Estella takes Leo's hand.

RODOLFO

smiles as tears fall from his eyes.

TONY AND ANGELINA

bow, hand-in-hand.

TONY

takes a bow. He motions to Angelina. She takes a bow.

Tony takes a final bow worthy of Chaplin's Little Tramp.

After a beat, he wipes away a single tear

```
from his cheek --

                    TONY
                 (singing)
            "La commedia e finita!"

The scrim falls in front of Tony and
Angelina. We see their silhouettes come
together in a kiss, and we --

FADE TO BLACK.

THE END.
```

Like Tony Pagliacci, we may learn that the beauty we are looking for is not behind us but inside us. We may discover that in order to possess this beauty we must reinvent ourselves, take chances, and break all the rules.

Injun
Ara Mgrdichian

baubles
trinkets
a bunch of beads

24 dollars.

i'll give you manhattan
and kill your children
slaughter all your women
and rape your brave men
with firewater and tobacco

reservation foreplay
casino recompense
casino prison
i'm the guard that will feed you
dear john letters
and pruno

i've got shivs to plant into
your raggedy junkie hands
when you must die

trinkets
baubles
a bunch of beads

full transgression

a betrayal
you will never be able to understand
even sitting there, bull,
upon a nest of your
forefathers' bones
contemplating your non-existence

sand mandala
spirit of the hawk
clipped wing
clipped life

i'll show you the life of the mind
as your dreams vibrate
through my hollow thickness

blood, blood, blood
all over my hands

and I'll still bring you back to life
to kill you
again and again

you are dead now
i've been dead forever

I, Lilith
Portia Putnam

You male scholars
Over millennia
Erased my place
As Wife of Adam.
You, envious
Of a woman,
Omitted me, then
Substituted for me as
First woman, Eve, the rib.
You mock nature,
Not recording the
Noble hymn of
Man and Woman,
Rising equal
From God's hand.
You drag Man down
By damning Woman.
I was not
Expelled from Eden
But planned my exit,
Keeping myself
Free from domination,
Leaving triumphant.

Meeting
Harold Pinter

It is the dead of night

The long dead look out towards
The new dead
Walking towards them

There is a soft heartbeat
As the dead embrace
Those who are long dead
And those of the new dead
Walking towards them

They cry and they kiss
As they meet again
For the first and last time

August 2002

Harold Pinter's *War*
M.C. Gardner

Harold Pinter's "Meeting" opens a slim volume including twelve of his poems. The collection is called *War*. With the exception of one piece, the poems were published in a variety of periodicals, chronologically from August 2002 to March 2003. They are published, along with a speech given at the University of Turin, by the publishing house of Faber and Faber.

War is a scream in the night that echoes down corridors of silence. Pinter rages with the futility of a latter-day prophet who knows that God is not only dead, but more frightfully, that he is an American who is deaf as well:

> And all the dead air is alive
> With the smell of America's God.

Several of the poems are obscene, as befits their subject:

> The big pricks are out.
> They'll fuck everything in sight.

Perhaps only Bertrand Russell, an English pacifist from early in the twentieth century, has fulminated as furiously as the English Pinter does here, early in the twenty-first: "…The U.S. administration is a bloodthirsty wild animal."

One feels in the next breath that Pinter might apologize to bloodthirsty wild animals for making the unseemly comparison.

In "Meeting," half of the poem's twelve lines contain the word "dead." There are the *long dead* and the *new dead*. The *long dead* is history. *We* are the *new dead* or, in the least, shall shortly be. Pinter's anger is directed at a world that has no patience for that inevitability.

His recent brush with mortality has eroded his patience further.

He won't let the horror of 9/11 excuse a doctrine that exploits *that* tragedy to further its own ends. From his speech at the University of Turin:

> *The hypocrisy behind its public declarations and its own actions is almost a joke. America believes that the 3,000 deaths in New York are the only deaths that count, the only deaths that matter. They are American deaths. Other deaths are unreal, abstract, of no consequence.... The atrocity in New York was predictable and inevitable. It was an act of retaliation against constant and systematic manifestations of state terrorism on the part of America over many years, in all parts of the world.*

Camus famously said, "At any street corner the feeling of the absurd can strike any man in the face." Pinter asserts such feeling is not restricted to America's latest belligerence or the 9/11 disasters that preceded it. T.S. Eliot would agree:

> Falling towers
> Jerusalem Athens Alexandria
> Vienna London
> Unreal

Playwright Donald Freed extends the poet's list:

> *From his earliest writings until his latest plays and poetry, the theme—explicit or implied, verbal or suggested in silences—has never swerved: human beings are so utterly vulnerable, so contingent on powers without pity, so scandalously naked to the techno-chemical fury of the twentieth century, that those who have a voice and a language must use it to create the record—by word in combination with unspeakable silence—of Buchenwald, Nagasaki, Vietnam, Chile, and Nicaragua. "*

The record of word, and the substance of silence is profoundly at work in his plays and so also here. Of silence Pinter once wrote:

> *There are two silences—one when no word is spoken. The other when perhaps a torrent of language is being employed. This speech is speaking of a language locked beneath it. That is its continual reference. The speech we hear is an indication of that which we don't hear.... When true silence falls we are still left with the echo but are near nakedness. One way of looking at speech is to say that it is a constant stratagem to cover nakedness.*

Out of his anger flows a torrent of jeremiads. America is the new Babylon. Invasions are word games disguised by the appellations *Freedom* and *Shield*.

From the end of "American Football":

> We blew them into fucking shit.
> They are eating it.
>
> Praise the Lord for all good things.
>
> We blew their balls into shards of dust,
> Into shards of fucking dust.
>
> We did it.
>
> Now I want you to come over here and kiss
>   me on the mouth.

August 1991

The reader will note that the date of the poem corresponds with the end of the first Gulf War. It could just as easily be read to signify the end of the second. In either it is clear that winning is a dubious endeavor. As William Faulkner observed, "...victory is an illusion of philosophers and fools."

The war goes on whether under the oppression of a dictator or under the pale of the American occupation. In either instance Americans and Iraqis die during the passage of each succeeding week. If a bomb blows off your arms it matters little to which side the ordnance belonged. The *liberators* are now subject to the same depleted uranium they used in their own weaponry. The weapons of mass destruction are our own. How many of the thousands of remaining troops will add their names to the thousands whose blood we left pooling in the desert?

There is a poignant loneliness to death in Pinter's poems. Faulkner was right: "…Christ was not crucified, he was worn away by a minute clicking of little wheels." George Bernard Shaw was right: "Death is not cumulative. There is only one death and it is our own."

The final poem of the collection is the only one not dated. In it he shows us our future—a bureaucratic voice makes formal inquiries of a deceased's remains. From the first and last stanzas of "Death"—

> Where was the dead body found?
> Who found the dead body?
> Was the dead body dead when found?
> How was the dead body found?
>
> …
>
> Did you wash the dead body
> Did you close both its eyes
> Did you bury the body
> Did you leave it abandoned
> Did you kiss the dead body

The final silence of "Did you kiss the dead body?" is the heartbreaking obverse of the angered irony of the earlier "kiss," quoted above. When we remember that the first poem of the collection, "Meeting," closes with, "They cry and they kiss / As they meet again / For the first and last time," we hear the faint echo of Rilke. We remember *Elegies* that sought *language where languages end*. We sense that Pinter's rage is book-ended by his humanity.

Those who do not condemn the atrocities wrought in their name are condemned in turn. Pinter's outrage was the most humane voice to arise from the Iraqi Wars. These poems are an unsettling commentary on the American and British enterprise. Jeremiah knew that Babylon was at the gate. He knew Jerusalem would fall and his people would call him traitor. Victory, defeat, and a prophet's silence—Pinter wrote "Weather Forecast" as the first bombs fell:

Weather Forecast

The day will get off to a cloudy start.
It will be quite chilly
But as the day progresses
The sun will come out
And the afternoon will be dry and warm.

In the evening the moon will shine
And be quite bright.
There will be, it has to be said,
A brisk wind
But it will die out by midnight.
Nothing further will happen.

This is the last forecast.

March 2003

Souls A'Burning
The Personal Correspondence between a Jewish Mother and a Black Bum
Kevin "Bumdog" Torres

Editors' Note:
This is a short adaptation of the first chapter of a novel. The selection is taken from Act 1.

Time:	*Late Morning*
Place:	*Fairfax District of Los Angeles, California*
Characters:	RUTH, *A middle-age Orthodox Jewish mother of four.*
	KEVIN, *A homeless black man.*
Setting:	RUTH *and* KEVIN *meet as* KEVIN *rifles through* RUTH*'s trash bins.*

RUTH: I'm sorry, what's your name?

KEVIN: Kevin.

RUTH: Mine's Ruth.

KEVIN: The pleasure is all mine

RUTH: Is there anything else you're going to need, Kevin?

KEVIN: No thanks, this is enough…. But can I ask you a question?

RUTH: What?

KEVIN: What are those things? (KEVIN *points up and above the audience.*) Those things, that look like huts. The ones with the plywood walls and palm tree branches for a roof. I've seen them pop up all over the neighborhood. Behind houses, on the side of houses, and in every single synagogue and Jewish school. I tried to ask this one Rabbi what it was, but he said it was too difficult to explain, I keep pestering him for an answer but he refused.

RUTH: That's a Sukka.

KEVIN: A what?

RUTH: A Sukka. You never heard that before?

KEVIN: No.

RUTH: A Sukka is a Jewish tradition that we have this time of year. For eight days we eat all our meals in it. It's to remind us of the forty years we spent in the desert. You see how it's made fairly flimsy. That's to remind us there is no real protection except God. And see the roof how it's made up of branches but not too many. That's so we can see through up to God. The whole purpose is to remind us of how difficult it was for our ancestors to reach the holy land. The poverty, pain, and sacrifice they endured to achieve God's purpose. Back in Detroit we don't have palm trees, so we used cypress trees. As a kid when I thought of Sukkas I always remember the smell of cypress.

KEVIN: That's beautiful.

RUTH: Yes, it is.

KEVIN: But if you really want to know what it was like living like they did why don't you live in the Sukka for eight days?

RUTH: Some people do. It depends on their tradition. I grew up in Detroit. And it's somewhat impractical to live in a Sukka at this time of year.

KEVIN: But isn't the purpose to make you realize the power of God to protect? To make you closer to God?

RUTH: Living in a Sukka in the middle of September in Northern Michigan will make you a lot more closer to the hypothermia ward at the county hospital. Although your point is still well taken.

KEVIN: I've been living in Sukkas off and on all my life but I didn't know it. I remember being able to look up at the roof through to the sky, but I never thought about God while I was doing it. I wish I had heard about these Sukkas before. I would have appreciated those spots more.

RUTH: It's never too late.

KEVIN: That's one of those sayings that I've heard more times than I've experienced.

RUTH: Don't tell me you've given up, Kevin.

KEVIN: I won't tell you that, but that's what's happened.

RUTH: You can't let that happen. There's a thing we call *menataza*. Basically it means your purpose for going on. God has a purpose for everyone even though we may not know what it is. But when you give up, you give up on God's divine plan and that's a mortal sin. I'll tell you something, there are days when I feel like jumping off a roof when I think about all the people in the world and what they do to each other. But the reason I don't is because my religion forbids it.

KEVIN: Be nice if I had a religion like that.

RUTH: What is your religion?

KEVIN: Nothing specific. My mother was something of a hippie. One week we'd be in a Catholic church, the next in a Buddhist temple, then she'd drag me to some damn place where people meditated all day surrounded by pictures of people levitating over fences. I pretty much have an open architecture when it comes to religion.... And what about you? Have you always been an Orthodox Jew?

One Father's Haiku
From Shtetl to Ultrasound
Lance Fogan

Voices stir within.

It Must Have Felt the Same for You, Too, Dad, Didn't It?

You were debonair imitating Fred Astaire a half century ago, tap dancing on our kitchen linoleum in your slippers and pajamas with a Lucky Strike cigarette between your lips. Doctors appeared in advertisements back then, promoting that Camels, Pall Malls, and Chesterfield cigarettes were so "mild for the 'T zone'"—the throat and tongue. I remember, after you began regular visits to our doctor, that our routine was for me to call out in a jocular fashion as you danced "Dad, your heart! Your heart!" ...

You were parked in the cab, waiting to start your first run of the night at Buffalo's New York Central Railway Station. You probably felt severe pre-sternal pressure pain, and then everything went black, as you died at age 46. The abnormal rhythm stopped your heart on November 9, 1953. Dr. W. had diagnosed angina pectoris—chest pain with exertion due to "hardening of the arteries"—during that past year. Bernie, your friend and fellow cabbie, rubbed snow on your chest, as he tried to help any way that he could. Then Mom got the call at home; I was a 14-year-old eighth grader. I'm still proudly wearing your Bar Mitzvah ring that was removed from your finger before we buried you.

Well, Dad, on May 31st, 2000, when I was 60, I had my heart attack. I confess I was anxious, and then relieved, when I made it past my own 46th birthday. I never smoked. I rode a stationary bike for 30 minutes four mornings each week for 16 years. In addition, I had been following a strict very low-fat diet ever since a chest-pain scare that led to an abnormal stress test with isotope cardiac scan nine years ago. The test indicated an area of low myocardial perfusion from a presumed partial coronary blockage. My doctors and I followed conservative management of the condition without an angiogram. Baby aspirin and a statin lipid-lowering drug were added to my anti-hypertensive at that time. The stress from my clinical neurology practice of recent years had decreased much of the previous enjoyment that I had derived from my work; fortunately I was able to retire at age 58. I love retirement. I love my family, especially my year-old first grandchild who lives with his parents just five minutes away. Holding that baby and kissing his head is my definition of happiness.

On that fateful morning when I "died," I awoke at 6:30 a.m. to start a much-anticipated day of sightseeing with out-of-town relatives. I performed my ablutions, took a baby aspirin and my antihypertensive medications. While on my stationary bike, however, I began to feel a substernal sensation. This wasn't alarming because so many different sensations (i.e. quick "pulls" in the chest, aches, and skipped heartbeats) had occurred so often, and disappeared in a second, that I considered them non-consequential. Vigorous activity and strains, such as hauling up and pulling in the sail on my windsurfer, have never caused these feelings. But, as I continued to exercise, the sensation became more intense, a mild pain now. It was even in my throat. "Well, I have a great day planned, let's hope that it stops," I thought. It didn't. I even reduced the tension to ease the peddling. Even though these symptoms signaled an ominous development, I carried on with my regimen. True to form, the most common first response to one's own heart attack is DENIAL!...

"My husband is having chest pain!" my wife said into the receiver, her voice trembling.... "What's your name, sir?" ...

Gazing up at my ceiling I thought, "I'm going to die! Well, I've lived a good life. I've had three wonderful years of retirement. I have provided for my family. So, if this is IT, then this is IT." It really seemed so easy to die. I'll have to remember that the next time....

It must have felt the same for you, Dad, didn't it?

Surging,

ledical Student Off to Jungle

By LANCE FOGAN

Journey to Mission
In Jungle Describe

BY LANCE FOGAN

Medical
student's
summer

in Papua

LEADING THE ADVENTURES of physicians who undertook medical missions to the more inaccessible corners of the world stirred the imagination of Lance Fogan, student at the State versity of New York School of Medicine, Buffalo. Last summer, his last carefree vacation time, he set about emulating the he admired.

Having obtained the post of "working guest" and assistant to only physician at a mission hospital in Papua, he drew out savings, raised more money, and, armed with a tropical sun text, stethoscope, camera and 13 inoculations, flew to v Guinea. From there it was a matter of hours till he was aged into a jungle clearing among stone age tribesmen one

IN OPERATING THEATER only screened room in St. Margaret's Hospital, Lance Fogan assisting amidst gazers in town of Samari old Papuan...

ON MORNING ROUNDS, Dr. Maurice L. Duvall, Australian trained... specialist, pauses between wards with Janet Trevelyan, English nur...

o Medical Stude
a Jungle Hospital

By Lance Fogan

ST. MARGARET'S Hospital in the name of four long, single-story buildings the Anglican Episcopal Mission at Samarai...

...practically by hand.

ebbing,

The Neurology in Shakespeare

Lance Fogan, MD, MPH

● William Shakespeare's 37 plays and poetry contain many references of interest for almost all of the medical specialties. To support that the Bard could be considered a Renaissance neurologist, the following important neurological phenomena have been selected from his repertoire for discussion: tremors, paralysis and stroke, sleep disturbances, epilepsy, dementia, encephalopathies, and the neurology of syphilis.

(Arch Neurol. 1989;46:922-924)

The factual information of Shakespeare's life would fill only half a page. He wrote a will; tax bills and a death certificate have his name on them. The rest of his life experiences are known from what others speculate. Yet, his works stand as evidence that he had an oceanic mind; one that observed, absorbed, and understood everything toward which he directed his attention. In the Elizabethan age, intelligent lay observers were as effective, if not at least less dangerous, in their ministrations to the sick as trained physicians. It is probably on this basis that Shakespeare, that great mirror held up to mankind, could so accurately describe the various signs, symptoms, and courses of disease.

TREMORS

There are several references to apparent paralysis agitans, or tremulous conditions, among the Bard's contingent of symptoms and diseases. Tremor in the senium is in *Troilus and Cressida* I,3,172: Ulysses says, "And then forsooth, the faint defects of age/ Must be the scene of mirth; to cough and spit,/And with a palsy fumbling on his gorget (armor),/Shake in and out the rivet ... " Shakespeare seems

Accepted for publication December 12, 1988.
From the Departments of Neurology, Kaiser Permanente Medical Center, Panorama City, Calif, and UCLA School of Medicine, Los Angeles.
Reprint requests to Department of Neurology, Kaiser Permanente Medical Center, 13652 Cantura St, Panorama City, CA 91402 (Dr Fogan).

to be describing paralysis agitans in Lord Say in *Part 2 Henry VI* IV, 7,84: Butcher queries, "Why dost thou quiver, man?" Lord Say responds, "The palsy, and not fear, provokes me." Then Jack Cade observes that Say's head shakes (as in paralysis agitans), "Nay, he nods at us, as who should say, 'I'll be even with you?' I'll see if his head will stand steadier on a pole ... behead him."

PARALYSIS

An enticing clinical description suggestive of stroke is offered by the incorrigible Falstaff in *Part 2 Henry IV* I,2,101: "And I hear ... his highness is fallen into this same whoreson apoplexy ... This apoplexy, as I take it, is a kind of lethargy, ... a kind of sleeping in the blood, ... a whoreson tingling ... It hath it original from much grief, from study and perturbation of the brain ... " Apoplexy is a "sudden stop of sense and voluntary motion, from an affection of the brains" according to Schmidt.[1] Later the King again suffers apoplexy in IV,4,110: the King says, " ... And now my sight fails, and my brain/Is giddy. O me! Come near me. Now I am much ill." Warwick responds, " ... You do know these fits/Are with his highness very ordinary./Stand from him, give him air, he'll straight be well ... " Gloucester adds, "This apoplexy will certain be his end." The King briefly recovers but shortly thereafter dies. No further useful mention is made of symptoms, focal or otherwise. We can speculate that he suffered from stroke and/or transient ischemic attacks and/or seizures. York, an old man in *Richard II*, has a palsied arm, which implies "paralysis, cessation of animal function."[1] In II,3,103: York says, " ... O' then how quickly should this arm of mine,/Now prisoner to the palsy, chastise thee ... "

In a passage from *Measure For Measure* III,1,34 the Duke expounds on the toils, stresses, and worthlessness of life, and refers to one of the features

of old
all thy
and o
eld ...

Sha
King
hunchb
This in
chronic
in ma
usurpat
hero, F
Shakesp
Elizabet
record,
Duchess,
in her tra
livered of
into this
ward"—a
arm was d
therewith
sleeve to h
where he s
arm, and su
describe the
street scene
Brachial ple
correlate wi
liveries; une
in a limp po
hemiparetic
gait that in t
a spinal cor
kyphoscoliosi
III,2,155: Ric
corrupt frail n
To shrink mir
shrub;/To ma
on my back,/V
mock my body;
unequal size;/f
every part ...
III,4,68: Richa
mine arm is l
withered up."

SLEEP AN

It is known th
tinue even durin
register exter
Shakespeare see
suggestion under

22   Arch Neurol—Vol 46, August 1989

surrounding.

For Perry, So He Will Know What He Did

JULY 1, 4:20 PM:
Your mommy, Aunt Sara, Bebe, you, and I landed in New York City to board the QE2 ocean liner the next day. I had been working with you for months with picture books, and discussions, so that you would understand and recognize NYC, London, and their many sites, the geography of our trip, and you certainly knew all about them when we got to those places. Landing at JFK, I knelt down to  your stroller and told you, "In New Yawhk, dey talk like dis." And you immediately started to robustly imitate that. You responded with great interest on my pointing out the bridges, tunnels, and tall buildings as we were driven into Manhattan.

6:25 PM: Upon entering the Sheraton's dining room for dinner, you immediately went over to a table where a single young woman was eating and you began to climb onto her adjoining chair and said "I'm going to sit here." We all laughed at your adorable nature. When your chocolate milk came, in a wine-type of glass, you said, "Here's my wine." Shortly after, you spilled it. NYC tour buses outside the hotel had the Statue of Liberty image on them. You identified it at first glance.

11:30 PM: You and I were the only two in our connecting hotel rooms still awake when we looked down on the street and saw so much activity at that time of night. You then understood, and repeated, that New York City is "the big apple," and "the city that never sleeps."

JULY 2, 2: 35 PM: We boarded the ship. As we left New York harbor you called out, "the Statue of Liberty."

6:20 PM: You attracted the attention of the waitresses passing our table in the Queen's Grill. On command, you further won their hearts with a wink, which you learned to do a long time ago. "I'm two" was your quick response to people's queries.

JULY 4, 2 PM: In the ship's library you recalled that your mommy earlier told you about the "adult section" and knew it differed from the "children's section." People were saying that you were so smart as you commented on the pictures in the books that we were perusing. You were afraid to go out on deck the first couple of days; that soon passed. At dance lessons, the woman instructor danced with you, to stop you from running amongst the dancers. You would imitate, "cha, cha, cha, one, two, three," with the proper timing.

6:30 PM: All the diners and staff were "awing," and smiling, and congratulating you as you marched into the restaurant properly tuxedoed and a blue binky-pacifier in your mouth. One woman said that you needed a black-colored binky to go with your formal outfit. You replied, "How're you doing?" to someone asking how you were, as your Daddy had taught

you. We beamed as the formally attired maitre de bowed, shaking your hand, and remarking, "You are looking very smart this evening, sir." Soon after we sat down for dinner, you would start pulling your hair and sucking on your binky, indicating that you were about to sleep. The waiters then set up a "bed" with two empty chairs next to our table, and we all were happy and relaxed for the next 2 hours. That happened every night.

9:30 PM: When I carried you in my arms, sleeping, from the restaurant, both of us in our tuxedoes, one man, with deep sincerity, said, "That is truly a beautiful sight."

JULY 5, 2 PM: I saw a pod of dolphins near the ship. You missed them and later you said to some young kids, "Big

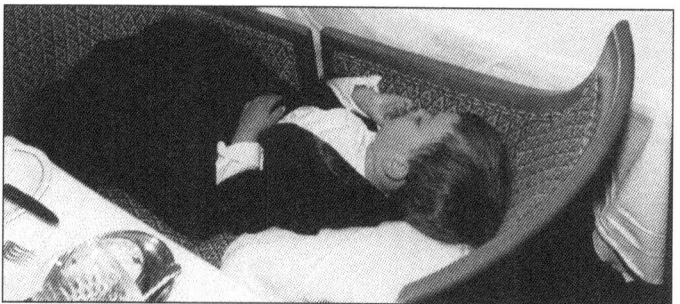

boy, where are the dolphins?" People on board were getting to know you. I wouldn't let them forget your name. I had it written on my shirt. Strangers would say, "There goes Perry and his Grandpa."

6 PM: At the captain's cocktail party, your tuxedo and happy demeanor even caught the captain's attention. He seemed delighted to bend down to give you a personal greeting and handshake. But, he didn't seem phased when you queried, as I had prompted you, "Captain, sir, please, may I see the bridge?" I had thought that he wouldn't be able to resist your brilliant request, and that we would all get an invitation to tour the QE 2's bridge, but, he smiled diplomatically, and greeted the next in line.

JULY 6, 10 PM: You again had fallen asleep at dinner but you awoke at 10 PM, raring to go. So you dressed and we went to the Midnight Buffet. On discussing our upcoming talent show performance, you repeated what I had told you, "If I don't face the audience we have to go back to our room?" As we walked through the gambling casino, you called the slot machines "banks."

JULY 7, 3:15 PM: You developed the hiccups as we walked to the afternoon talent show, and I worried that you wouldn't be able to go on. When we got to the Grand Lounge for the show, the young women organizers got so excited, laughing, actually screaming, upon seeing you formally dressed, and I knew that we were going to be hot. I had requested that we be the first act as I feared that if we were delayed, you, a two-year old, would get bored, or become otherwise occupied, and not want to go on. No one else was aware that you still were in diapers under your tux. The MC introduced us as "Perry and His Grandpa from Valencia, CA, singing the Ink Spots' 'Java Jive.'" You strode right up onto center stage with me without hesitation. When I leaned down and told you to do the intro, you grabbed the microphone close to your mouth and belted it out. Flashbulbs, laughter, and applause accompanied our singing. Even the backup band members behind us on the stage were broadly smiling.

At the end we got rousing applause from the 150-200 in attendance. You bowed your head so sweetly, and said "Thank you, audience," as I had taught you. You got a Cunard stuffed dog, and we each got a certificate; those will be framed so that you'll have it to show to your own grandchildren 50 years from now.

JULY 8, 9 AM: A man said the words to our song, "A cup, a cup, a cup," recognizing us, as we walked by. Another lady congratulated you on your performance on the previous day, but you turned away, shyly. At dockside in Southampton, a woman told me, as I held you, "He's the sweetest little boy." Another lady came up to us and with heartfelt sincerity said, "Thank you for the joy." In fact, the older people, throughout the voyage, smiled and laughed at your many antics in the Queen's Room during dance lessons, or at tea time.

You make so many people happy just by being you.

I am found again.

We Only Kill Our Friends
A Novel in Progress
William Wasz

CHAPTER I

NEW FISH

The heat pounded down on me—giant hammer blows that never seemed to end.

Nine months of the year, the average temperature hovered at one hundred fifteen degrees, so intense that simple breathing became a laborious repetition. On that desolate, sterile prison yard prisoners stood idle, barely moving. Sweat dripped from every pore of their tattooed and scarred bodies. Ever present for each was the knowledge that at least one of their peers wished their demise; this left them always on alert. A man-made Hades it was, complete with a thermal environment to underscore the insanity.

I watched cautiously, fully aware that I was what prisoners called a "fish," an inmate new to the "system," someone mostly ignorant of the ways, culture, and terminology of the men around him. Forever doomed to a life filled with drugs, hate, and never-ending violence.

Slowly, I came to realize that the system had sent me to this particular place as retribution. An indirect message, stating that my crimes were sole cause for this placement: straight to a place where society built and housed indiscriminate hatred, racism, and death, and all in the name of "corrections," a "Level 4" maximum-security institution, Calipatria State Prison, a few miles from the Mexican border, a facility that the State of California regards as a place of "justice and rehabilitation."

On one side of the short, oval walking track circling the prison yard, two groups of Black inmates, the Crips street gang, and their rivals, the Bloods, stood watch continuously over one another. Each gang constantly anticipated a *move* by the other. *Move* meant attacking. This was only one facet of the watch, for both also had to observe the *Southern Mexican* gang:

A gang dedicated to launching attacks against the Blacks at any indiscretion they deemed a violation of their own warped code. A mad irony: Crips and Bloods, rivals for eternity, unite only to do battle with the Southern Mexicans.

A group of more than one hundred Southern Mexicans stood only a few yards to the left of the blacks on the oval track. The name of the city, street, or area that they came from adorned each of their bodies, permanently tattooed into their skin: street gang insignias, proclamations of turf. Most tried to consistently maintain a *hard core* look in order to intimidate the smaller or younger members of their group. Large moustaches and well-developed upper torsos further bolstered their *machismo*. Machismo was a carefully cultivated aspect of their physical presence, their masculinity and strength betraying no sign of weakness to anyone.

A warped logic surrounded me when I sat with my new *people*, the infamous Aryan Brotherhood. The membership was a select few, but a group that most whites found it necessary to congregate around, in order to display their unity. A superficial unity, because once the surface was scratched, the core turned out to be a union of drug addicted dope fiends... As I sat there among my newfound *friends*, I felt as if I were baking in a pizza oven. Silently, I listened to countless prison war stories, all told by tattoo-covered preachers of false supremacy. Some were in fact stone cold killers, this I could tell simply by looking at them; killers that even Hollywood would have a hard time conjuring up.

An incident construed as a gesture of disrespect had been perpetrated against the Southern Mexicans. A soccer ball had landed on the Blacks' side of the weight lifting area, causing a Southern Mexican youngster to retrieve it. No race was allowed to enter another's territory. Words were exchanged. Both sides retreated, for contemplation time.

A decision was made by the Mexican *shotcaller*. That act of verbal disrespect could not go unchallenged. The *shotcaller* was a burly older member of the Mexican Mafia, so his decision was law. Slightly more than a dozen youngsters were delegated to dig up knives buried in different locations throughout the prison yard. Their objective, to stab as many Blacks as they could: kill them, if possible, but to "put holes in everyone they could get near." So, it was: a decision by one man, who would not even be a participant. He simply stood against a wall of the handball court, calmly observing his *soldiers* digging up the knives. Groups of three went to the area where a knife was buried and feigned a conversation as one squatted down and dug it up; all the while trying not to be noticed by the gunners posted in towers surrounding the yard... I glanced up at the main gun tower... With a clear view of the entire yard, the guard manning it acted as if he were completely ignorant of the actions below. He turned his head to the opposite side of the yard, he leaned out of the tower window. At that point, I assumed he was simply unaware of what was going on.

With venomous rage, they struck out with their weapons, trying to kill or maim. Those few seconds seemed like an eternity as groups converged. Blows from fists, stabs from knives... blood poured... Suddenly, a sharp report echoed from the first shot of the AR-14 rifles... a small explosion erupted in his skin. A combination of flesh, bone, blood instantly flew from his shoulder, his arms spreading out in a feeble effort to retain his balance. Shocked disbelief swept his face as he hit the ground, hard...

At that moment the full impact hit me: I had a twenty-year sentence and this would be my life for at least the next ten years...

The Conversation
Mary Gilvarry

Time:	*September 4, 2002*
Place:	*Split Locale: Los Angeles and Caherciveen*
Characters:	MARY, *an elderly woman, in Los Angeles.*
	EILEEN, *slightly younger woman,* MARY*'s cousin in Ireland.*
Setting:	MARY *at a computer.*
	EILEEN *at a kitchen table.*

MARY: It's disillusioning, isn't it—the priests—this sex abuse scandal?

EILEEN: It's certainly terrible. It's not only in America, but here in Ireland and in Australia. It's all because they don't have enough to do. Why, they often have only two Masses a week; the priests here just don't know what to do with themselves.

MARY: I remember when I was young. They seemed so elevated and I so low down in all the important ways. I could scarcely get breath to talk to them. I was so scared and so awed.

EILEEN: Until just recently, I thought they just couldn't do anything wrong. As God's agents, they just couldn't. Ah, but they've had the easy life. They haven't had to do like all the boys and men who've had to pack up and go to England and try to make out from scratch.

MARY: *(Laughs.)* You can get that an Irish country boy in London or Manchester would have a hard time of it. Their brogue would single them out.

EILEEN: I'm scared right now. Here in South Kerry, it's been raining all of May and June. Today it's dry but rain's forecast for tomorrow and the rest of July. The plants are rotting in the fields. Here in South Kerry there'll be suffering, we'll have to buy more of our food. Most of the farms here, you know, are little plots. They only have 8 to 10 cows at the most. The husband and the wife have to get some kind of jobs at the creamery or somewhere locally in order to live. They'll survive but it'll be hard. There hasn't been this much rain in a hundred years.

MARY: Ahh, Ireland's been terrible on its people. How many have survived in your family? Do you have a sister living?

EILEEN: No. So many of the children died even when they had just grown up. I told you that your mother's three brothers died here in their twenties.

MARY: You said, right, that two of them had to go into the *work house*. (*Pause.*) Is it that they couldn't make a living for themselves?

EILEEN: That's right, Mary. And that's why you have to pray. Pray that prayer, the Caplet for the Holy Souls, that I sent you. You need to go to Mass, Mary, and often. Forget about the priests. Praise the Lord. May the Blessed Mother look after you. God bless you, Mary, did you get that little job at the Church?

MARY: No, I didn't. Gee, I wish Johnnie were still around. Like me, he'd appreciate the irony of the priests bringing down the Church. He'd understand why I'm bereft about it. I'm old. I think we'd better end this conversation. It'll cost you too much, Eileen. God bless you, too. I'll pray for you.

> (*The voices cease. The telephones click back in their receivers. Both women stare into space. Lights fade.*)

Out of Focus
A Novel in Progress
Adrienne Nater

Chapter I—1990

The door closes. A figure stands, arms crossed, staring. The carpet is white: the walls are white, the drapes are white, the ceiling is white, the shelving is white. The mirror is dark: mementos pile up, surfaces overflow with books, trophies, photo albums. Family photographs stare into the room. Nothing moves. Nothing sounds.

Moves. Eleven steps. Stops. Looks down. The desk: white shaded lamp, left; typewriter, center: pen, pencil, paper, right. Top center, clock and calendar: October 9th, 1:43 PM. Outside, Southern California. Inside, cold shadows.

The bookcase. Eyes scan the titles. Pulls a book from the third shelf, reads the title, puts the book back. Turns again. White walls. Family photos, floor to ceiling. Hands stroke the photo albums, scrapbooks, mementos. Sits on the arm of the sofa, pulls out an album at random, opens, views the faces, places—closes.

Back to the desk. Sits. The weight presses her into the chair. 1:46 PM. Fingers rest on the keyboard: reaches to the right, picks up a black pen and a blank piece of lined paper.

Writes the date at the upper right; only the date, nothing more. Script neat, small and precise: each letter, each number, definable, uncannily familiar. The lack of style is the style.

Pushes the chair back, stands, and stumbles to the door. Fingers grip the handle, pressing downward. Opens the door, hesitates. Right hand reaches out. The photograph is seventy-five years old. Fingers trace two figures. Smiles, nods her head, turns away, closes the door.

And now she walks down the hall staring at her feet, her walk, familiar, strangely familiar, and moves through the living room, into the kitchen to the refrigerator and opens the door, reaches for the bottom shelf and grabs a can of beer and then opens the freezer and finds a cold glass, opens the can, pours and throws the can into the recycle bin and walks across the room to her armchair and sits with her feet up resting on the hassock. Then she takes out a cigarette, picks up the lighter, flicks the lighter, all the while watching her hands, lifts the glass and takes a long drink, and leans back. She closes and opens her eyes and watches the smoke drift out the window. Her glass is half empty.

She walked to the open front door, shrugged her shoulders, pushed open the screen door that's never locked and stepped outside. She saw the roses. She walked across the gravel-covered yard, head down, each step creating a grinding sound. She turned around, tilted her head up and gazed at the house. Then she placed her right hand on the tree for support, lowered herself to the ground and sat with her back against the trunk of the Magnolia.

Beneath her were the sharp uneven rocks. She closed her eyes and gathered her legs under the robe, wrapping her arms around her knees. She was still, listening. *"Alice, get my checkbook! I'll write you a check right now and we will—" "But that's $10,000 dollars!"*

It started to come back to her. The narrow road, the rocks, the barbed wire fencing, the endless expanse of weeds, the wild vines, wild gum and pepper trees, yellow flowering mustard. She looked down, picked up one of the jagged rocks, traced a rectangle in the dirt, heard old Ray, the builder— *"Run the chalk line and let's get started on the measurements. 1,100 square feet, slab foundation, cedar exterior, 1x12' planks, two fireplaces, gray slate entry, white frame windows and the usual fixtures."*

Her eyes flashed open and she saw the house: gray cedar planking, gray roof, two white chimneys, gray slate entryway, white framed windows: Twenty years. She looked up through the leaves into the blue. Placed her right hand on the ground for support, stretched out her legs and pushed to a kneeling position. A branch of the tree touched her head. She took a deep breath of the air. "What is it?" Who? Barbecue. No, onions and cloves with smoke flavor: Something, someone moves into her line of sight, near the barn entrance. "Where can I go?"

Unaware of the sunlight, she begins to walk, small careful steps to the orchard gate. Her hands automatically reaching forward to lift the cane latch. It strikes the adjoining fence with a sound so familiar that the goats don't notice as they rush toward her.

"One, two, three, four." She was counting her steps up the path. Counting each stride, "41, 42, 43" — "101, 102 103," until she reached 247. The trees on either side of the path formed a sanctuary as she walked. She reached the chain-link fence and gate at the northern boundary of the property, stood and stared, focusing on the 1888 farmhouse. She doesn't hear the trees rustling, the voices are too clear now: *"Wish the old man who bought the place would keep up the old homestead." "I'll bring the tractor for the heavy field work." "You like potatoes? We'll bring you some from the harvest." "Them pigs is boars, girls." "Why would you want to live in the country?"*

She lowers herself to the ground, supported by the hand over hand grasp she has on the fence wire. On her knees now, her head buried in her hands, elbows on the ground, she didn't feel the sweat rolling down her body. Crawled to the shelter of one of the trees, sat, her legs stretched out in front of her, her arms and hands out to the side.

Her eyes open, her gaze fixed, watching the path, framing the scene. *"Is that someone standing in the orchard?"* She sees a tall figure with thick wavy gray hair, dressed in white pants, white silk shirt, white shoes, Armanis? She calls out, "Hello, there." The sound of her own voice frightens her; she moves to get up. The figure disappears.

She drops back down into the thick layers of leaves, breathes in the earth's aroma. A warm comforting feeling is by her side, a weight across her left shoulder—"Mac, is that you?"

Mac, you wonderful dog, you are a comfort. "Comfort." She speaks the word aloud. But, then, at this exact moment, in the filtered sunlight, she is determined not to think of words. She strokes Mac's head and shoulders, closes her eyes, drifts back. Signs to the left, signs to the right. She sees people, places, objects; days and nights pass by. She feels hot, then cold, wet then dry. Sun, moon and stars blend into one glow. She listens: sounds are missing, voices are silenced, the noise is of the silence. She recognizes, one after the other, the streets and avenues. She hears herself pronouncing the words on the road signs.

She has been down each one and back again. Is it her feet that are traveling so fast and easy along the road? She senses no contact or resistance. Then she wonders: *am I the one in motion or is the road moving by my stationary body?*

Her eyes open and close again. Leaves, bark, cobwebs. Then, she is back living in Los Angeles, when it was a sleepy, sprawling town, more then sixty years past. 1937, Myra Street.

Chapter 2—1937

She stands there looking up at the craftsman house. It is a cloudless day, the first in months, in the spring of the year. She will begin public school in the fall.

Her thoughts of the dark winter times have faded. She is out of doors, in the shadow of the parkway tree, looking to her right and left, up at the branches of the tree, then down to see a pair of roller skates dangling in her right hand, her fingers wrapped around the leather straps. On the end of each strap is a buckle. The straps are attached to her skates. The shiny metal ball-bearing wheels are still, waiting. On her feet are loose-laced Buster Brown heavy-duty shoes: reinforced metal tips covering the toes, metal plates on the soles, both front and back. But, something is missing. She reaches up and touches her chest. Her skate key! It should be on a string hanging around her neck. In a flash she knows who has it. Where is he? He is not anywhere around! Not in the house, or the back yard, or in the garage. No! He is skating! She is not!

She is furious, so furious that she begins shouting and continues to shout his name, "Shelly! Shel-ly, where are you? Bring back my skate key! Shelly, I know you took it, bring it back! Now! SHELLY!"

She looks at the unscreened window of the house, expecting to see a face, see the front door open. She waits, she looks, and when no face appears, she pictures each of the three faces that could appear.

Thinking: *Now if a brown face with black hair appears it would smile at me, disappear, open the front door, walk to my side with soft said wise words. If a brown-haired white face appears, there would be a smile, a nod, the front door would open gently, and this one would also move to me, to comfort and embrace me with reassuring arms. But, if a white face with blond hair appears there would be no smile. The pale face would disappear, the front door would be thrown open, and I would hear the sound of my name shouted from the porch in accusing tones.*

Her first choice, the one she hoped to see at the window, was the brown face of Mae. Mae would move to open the front door, step across the porch, down the grassy path, to the sidewalk, and say, "Child, what are you squalling 'bout? If you needs somethin', go and get it direct, your shoutin' won't do a thing but exercise your mouth. Your mom won't have none of this shoutin' neither. Don't wake her up, make her upset."

Then I would say, "I'll quit shouting! But Shelly has the skate key. My skate key! I know he does. He can't find his. He is so stupid but he knows that without a skate key I can't keep the skates on my shoes. He's mean and selfish. Besides that he walks funny, big flat feet that point out like a duck's. I don't know why he has to live with us. You and Mommy and I should be on our own. Shelly and his mom don't need to live here." And Mae would say, "Child, just get on with your business."

Second choice was the white face with the brown hair. Not only would she smile from the window—it would be a worried smile, but still a smile—she would come out of the house, down the steps to the sidewalk, consoling, "Sh, sh, sh, don't shout, you'll wake your mother. Tell Aunt Willa what's wrong." I would tell her and then she would say, "Take my hand, baby, we'll walk together. Let's go and find Shelly and your skate key. Here, let me carry your skates. You're so little to be skating let alone searching around the block by yourself."

Her non-choice was the face she did not want to see: the white face with the blond hair; and no telling what would happen if she came out of the house. *Look out* me and *look out* Shelly!

Someone is home. Someone is always home: but no face comes to the window, no one opens the door, and nobody comes out onto the front porch or down the path. "Skate key" has become more important then any other word; it is the only meaningful word that relates to an object of the highest value in her right-now life. Without it she is stranded. With it she could travel—going every place in general, but no place in particular. Her mouth is set in a tight, determined expression. She knows what she must do, what she expects of herself: The plan is simple. Find Shelly! Get the skate key!

First she puts her skates on the cement sidewalk. With both hands free she pulls up her socks, reties and double-bows her shoelaces, smoothes down her dress, sweeps her long dark curls away from her face, grabs her skates by their straps, and sets out marching along the sidewalk, down the street, moving toward the corner, chanting "Step on the cracks, Step on the cracks!" Pauses.

Or is it "Don't step on the cracks?" She is kicking at stones with her steel-tipped shoes, swinging her skates by their long buckle-ended straps trying to remember the rest of the verse.

Even before she can reach the corner she hears the sound of a truck. It must be Wednesday! And there it comes. Moving along. Stopping at each home's curbside.

The two black garbage collector men are about their business; one is driving, the other standing on a shelf that is attached to the right side of the tailgate. Gracefully he reaches out with his right arm, his hand grabs the bail of the bucket; in a nimble effortless movement the bucket is swinging in an arc over the back of the truck, the contents spilling out on the already high pile of garbage, disturbing only the flies that follow and ride along for the entire trip, and the pail, back on the curb only inches from its original position.

She is always amazed watching their skill and efficiency. The men are her friends. Each week she helps to put the garbage pail at the curb. Each week she waves to the men and each week they shout at her, smiling back.

She remembers her focus, her mission: finding Shelly and the skate key. Now, where would he be? Not at the corner house. No. The German family lives there. I like the lady; she makes pickled pig's feet. We're not supposed to go into the house. Not to reach into the giant brine filled jar with our hands. Not to eat the pig's feet. I don't know why. I do talk to the lady, I reach into the jar, get one of the pig's feet—that is, whenever no one is around to tell on me and that no one is Shelly. And where is that big tattletale crybaby?

She walks on and on, up the street, peering into each yard. There are trees in the front yards and shade, lots of shade. Cool dark shade. She decides to rest and think away from the glare of the cement sidewalk. She puts her skates down by the elm tree trunk, plops down, sitting with her legs crossed Indian fashion, all but disappearing into the shadows.

She reasons. *I need to be ready.* When I find Shelly, how will I get my skate key? What would Mae say? I know, "Take care of your business. Do what you have to do." Aunt Willa would tell me that kindness is the best way. Be polite. Just walk up to him and say please, that you need the skate key and that we can share.

But, what if that doesn't work? I will be like mother. I will step out in front of him, plant my feet, my hands on my hips, give him the hard eye, put out my hand and wiggle my finger. Just stand, stare, wiggle that finger and wait. Which one?

And, then, she hears the sound of metal skate wheels grinding on the sidewalk. There he is! She does not move. She is watching him come closer. He rolls down the sidewalk. The key is dangling from its cord in his hand. She waits. Silently, she moves. Now she is standing. She has picked up her skates. They are hanging from her hands at the end on their straps. He is just about to whiz past. Out she jumps, yelling "Shelly, you stop right here, give me back my skate key!" He is so startled that he doesn't see the crack in the sidewalk. It catches one of the skate wheels and zippo: he turns into a sack of spilled beans, all over the place, on his back like a turtle.

One skate is flopping around his ankle. The other is still attached to his shoe. She is standing over him. Her tiny figure is hovering over his large body. He twists and turns and manages to rise to a standing, lopsided position.

"Give it to me!" She points to the object of her desire. The next moment she is on the ground.

Darkness overwhelms her: Stars flash, oceans roar, bells ring. Then silence. She regains her senses. She is surprised to find the sidewalk so close. Her head is throbbing. Her mouth hurts. She puts her free hand to the back of her head. There is an egg-size lump. She rubs the lump. She licks her lips. The taste is awful. She rolls over to her left side and manages to get herself to a sitting position. She moves her head from side to side, looks around. She is alone. It comes back. She had been reaching for her skate key. Shelly had pushed her. Where was he? She crawls over to the grass and into the shade. Her head is throbbing.

She thinks. *If I were Shelly where would I be right now? What would I be doing? Hum, if I were Shelly. I'd be hiding. Not too far away, but close by. Close enough to see me but unseen by me. So.* She looked around and saw a perfect place for observation and conceal-ment. It had to be the porch of this house.

That's where she would've hidden. But, she knew what he

did not; that this front porch had only one entrance and one exit to the street. It would be a trap. If he were hiding there she would have to surprise him. He mustn't get away. He still had the skate key and now she had another score to settle.

She got up without even a glance at the porch, walked a bit further up the street. Then, hidden by big bushes, she dashed up the neighboring driveway, crouching in the protection of the dense shrubs. Nothing hurt! She surveyed the lay of the land between herself and the porch. Figured that crawling next to the house, screened behind the bushes, would conceal her until the final dash.

She begins a careful, sightless, soundless move back through the skate-key battlefield and closer to the Shellycave. She is stealth itself.

When she reaches the edge of the porch she pauses. Peeks over from behind the red Camellia and let her eyes become accustomed to the darker interior. She could see Shelly.

She could make out his crouched figure at the far end of the porch, his attention directed toward the street side. Just keep it that way, fool, she is thinking as she picked up a dirt clod and then, barely moving her body, tossed it out to the street side of the house.

Shelly leaned forward, peering in the direction of the sound. She made her move!

Stooped over, feet moving, head low, she scurried around from the corner of the porch to the entrance. Up the steps, to his corner, it took her just a few seconds, now she was the one hovering. Her hand was out. "Give me my skate key!" He tried to get to his feet. Not this time!

Swish! Womp! Smack! Somehow the skates, still gripped by their ankle straps, have come to life. They know how to "take care of their business." His head is bowed and bloody, his feet are moving, the skate key is on the ground. He's crying. He's running. He's bleeding. He's screaming. "I'm gonna tell, I'm telling. My mom, your mom, they're gonna get you. Just wait 'til you get home. You'll be sorry!" He's down the steps of the porch, across the yard and up the street; she had never seen him move so fast. She hadn't thought that it was possible with flat duck feet.

With great calm, dignity, and pleasure, she retrieves the dropped skate key. Sitting on the top step of the porch steps:

she places her skates on the ground, slips her heavy-duty shoes onto the metal platforms. She positions the closed wrench end of the skate key on the toe-tightening bolt. The toe holders glide into position between the shoe tops where they meet the sole. She turns the mechanism until she is sure that the skates are on for the duration. She looks down at her feet. She smiles and thinks aloud, *I'm on my way!*

She slides her bottom down one step; she stands; looks up as she suspends the skate key necklace over her head. The string becomes a rainbow-colored ribbon, the skate key a silver star that glistens in the sunlight. She lowers her medal of valor, lets the ribbon settle on her shoulders, runs her fingers along the material, the emblem comes to rest on her chest. With great ceremony she strokes her medal and then, as she has been taught, transfers the key from front to back. She takes her first steps and then glides onto the surface of the smooth pavement, feeling like the winged horse in her storybook.

But she didn't get far before the picture of Shelly, his face covered with blood, floats up before her. She had—*no, the skates* had—cut his forehead open above his right eye. The magic skates became heavy, her feet and legs became wooden, uncooperative.

She tumbled off of her raceway onto the grass: *I didn't want to hurt him so much. The skates did it! I did it too. We did it.*

She can feel her legs and feet come back to life. She zips up the street, around the corner; waves to no one, stops for no one. And there she is in front of her house and there he is. Crying, bleeding, pointing. Mother, Aunt Jean, Aunt Willa, and Mae appear.

There is enough ice for the both of them. They sat on the sofa nursing their wounds, he on one end and she on the other. An ice pack on the front of his head, an ice pack on the back of hers.

They sat there alone for a long time. Boredom. He looked miserable, the girl thoughtful. So, then, she glanced over to his defeated figure and said softly: "Shelly, hey, Shelly, want to go skating?"

The Knock
James Ragan

He had known the neighbor's wife through veils,
a cliche she wore like the glance they'd trade
when passing down the front yard steps,
a foreign phrase she hadn't turned in greetings
but rehearsed in silence, nonetheless.

And always on the bus they'd take
to sitting opposite, staring up the threads of their eyes
toward some distant thought their minds had turned
like a skewer, perhaps, to braise the meat
of envy, a heartbeat less than hate. Of course,

there was her husband whom he never met
except in pubs where, back to back, he might attempt
a nod in deference to the passing of a beer
or soccer point that shouted past the video screen.
But while her husband chose to serve, a colonel,

he without the nerve, a stacking clerk,
had built a tedium of scorn into his life,
a boundary like the language neither would cross.
Until the knock, its force had savaged down her door;
the neighbor's wife he'd come to take

was dressing lampshades in Queen Anne's lace,
and, braving habit, dropped the needled cushion
to rush the veil up, as if the sainted silk
were a buckram to shield her from invasion,
the pins no dagger to his face or the country of his hate.

I'm a Man
Richard T. Hellinga

Take this chick I'm about to pass on the sidewalk. Big tits. Big hair. Yes, big hair, I like a nice mane to tug on when I'm coming from behind. Yeah-heah. I've got to tell Pete about her. Decent face, but not great, but who cares? It's not the face you fuck but the fuck you face, and I swear I've never had or wanted a fuck I couldn't face. That's what it comes down to. All I want to do is fuck. Fat or skinny, ugly or beautiful, drunk or straight. I just go for the fuck. Each new chick is like a new country, full of new hills and mountains and passes and ports of entry!

And take this dork walking behind her. He's not even looking at her! How can he not with the prime view he's got? Must be a fag. Only a fag wouldn't appreciate such a fine female specimen in full view.

We don't make eye contact; the big-breasted big-haired chick and I. I look up at the sky so that she doesn't think I'm gawking at her. Just some small clouds. The rest is clear blue and bright sun. Back to her. She's wearing shorts. That's one of the great things about Spring: when the legs come out. Legs Spring Eternal! Yeah, I got something ready to spring for you. I shift my notebook and paperback copy of *The Sun Also Rises* from my right hand to my left, so she'll think that a guy like me has some sophistication. Though I still have to finish reading the book for my Hemingway paper. A real man's writer. I keep my pace slow. We pass each other and I take a casual glance at her back side. Nice legs under those light blue shorts. Christ, that dork's got a Dukakis button on his backpack. What a loser. The election's been over for like six months and your pussy candidate lost, you idiot. Get over it. Bush won. Reagan's man.... They all want it. Maybe not now. But eventually they will. But you have to catch them in that mood, or put them in it, make them want it. When they demand the fuck.

Just like that fat chick last weekend. She was drunk and I was drunk and I told her she was the kind of girl I could fall in love with, the kind of stupid line that only works when you're drunk. But she was a wet-n'-wild ride. Sloppy drunk sex. Then as soon as she passed out I made my escape. Maybe I'll fuck her again. I don't know, nah, we'll see... The chick with the blue shorts and the mane has got what I want. Pussy Galore. Not gay-lord. Like that porn Pete and I watched the other day, "The Erotic Adventures of Pinocchio." To our own circle jerk— "It's Not His Nose that Grows," should've been the subtitle.

Time for lunch with Pete. Where we always hang out. Pete and scoping out some chicks. Hope we can get our regular spot. Then theater class, to scope out some more chicks. All the guys in there are fags or pussies or dorks, so I stand out. I swear I'm the only real man in the entire class. That goes for the fag teacher, too. Besides, some lines from Shakespeare are good to know. Chicks go for that romantic shit. "Drink is a provoker of three things, it provokes and unprovokes, it provokes the desire but takes it away... it sets him on and gets him off; makes him stand to and stand out. "Whatever. Yeah, I bet Shakespeare got plenty of those Elizabethan chicks. Lesbian chicks. Lesbos. Two hot chicks goin' at it.

I walk into the Burger King. Actually, it's pretty cool that we've got one on the campus instead of some lame-ass cafeteria with crap food. Pete's already here, sitting by the window, yes, our usual spot, which makes it convenient to view chicks both inside and outside. We've spent many hours watching lots of chicks at that table. It's practically ours. When I get to NIU I'm going to need to find a whole new prime chick-watching spot like this. Pete's a year older than me but he dropped out of high school, then later got his GED and started taking classes with me. I go over to where he's sitting and put my stuff on the chair across from him.

"What's up, Martin?" asks Pete, his head still down as he's reading the textbook he's got spread out flat on the table. Can't tell which class it's for. He's looking good today. The top buttons of his shirt are open.... He works out a lot. We work out together. He's wearing his cologne. Drakkar Noir. We never go anywhere without being showered, freshly shaven, and cologned up. You never know when the opportunity to fuck is going to come up. So you have to be ready for PP (Potential Pussy). No second chances.

"Just saw this hot chick in blue shorts," I say.

"Dark hair?"

"Yep."

He turns the page and nods. "Saw her leave here a minute

ago. She's totally hot. I'd do her."

"Definitely. But other than that, same old shit. How 'bout you?"

"Nothing new, man, nothing new."

"I'm going to get something to eat."

"I'll watch your stuff."

The line's long but it's moving at a decent pace. My stomach is rumbling. There's a guy and two girls behind the registers taking orders. That guy is there all the time. He's skinny and dorky-lookin'. The black chick is kinda hot, but only a model like Cindy Crawford could look good in those ugly-ass uniforms. The white chick is kinda cute. She looks new. I think she's checkin' me out. I'd do her. If she takes my order I'm going to make my move. Tell her I bet she looks good without the uniform. No. You look good *despite* that uniform. No. You look good *in* that uniform. No, that's stupid. You make that uniform look *good*. No, that won't work. God-dammit. I'm getting closer to her. Think of something. She probably sees a couple hundred guys a day in here. I've got to be able to say something that's really clever. One, two, three, four, looks like she'll be the one that takes *my* order. Yeah-heah. I'd like two naked breasts and a wet pussy, please.... Christ, I can't say that. They'll throw me out. It's a burger joint not a brothel. Though I bet a brothel on a college campus would be a goldmine. "For what our natures do pursue." That would be awesome, to be able to fuck before, in-between, and after classes. Fuck is a good-sounding word. One hard syllable. It's like the perfect word for what it describes. The insertion. Fast and firm. In and out. Fuck-fuck, fuck-fuck. Tick-tock, tick-tock. Here we go. Faster and faster. Until the ultimate point of pleasure is reached. All right. Calm down. Think, Martin. Think. You're walking up to her register. PP at 12 o'clock.

"Welcome to Burger King, may I please take your order," she says.

All right. I've got it. I know just what to say to turn her on. "You know, I think you'd look better without that uniform."

She rolls her eyes. They're green. Man, I can't remember the last time I've seen a green-eyed chick. She takes one of those heavy sighs and she's gripping both sides of the register. Shit, that didn't come out right. Fuck. I fucked up. Mayday. Mayday. Going down. And not in the good way.

"I meant that I'd like to see you some time without that uniform," I say.

She's tapping one side of the register with her nails real hard. Shit. That didn't come out right either. "I'm working," she says like some serious grade school teacher. "And you're getting in the way. So either order some food or leave."

I'm feeling warm. Embarrassed warm. My hands are clammy now and I need to pee. Must've been that Coke I drank in Accounting class. "I'm sorry. I'll have a Whopper with cheese, an order of large fries, and a large coke."

"Is that for here or *to go?*"

"Uh, for here."

She punches it into the register and tells me the total. I go to give her the money, but her hands are on the register. I'm holding the money out to her. She's staring at me like I'm some sort of moron. Fuck if she isn't right. I'm usually slicker than that. More clever than that. But she won't reach out a hand for the money. So I set the money on the metal counter. As soon as my hand is away she takes it, counts it, punches it in, puts it in the drawer, counts the change, tears off the receipt, sets the change and the receipt on the counter, and moves her hand away real quick. It's like she thinks I've got AIDS or something. Fuckin' paranoid. I just want to fuck her, not kill her. Some chicks just don't get it. She could be more forgiving. But she's not. She should understand how any guy could screw up in front of her like I just did. But she obviously doesn't. Some Shakespeare would've worked better. "Thou has frighted the word out of his right sense, so forceful is thy wit." Definitely. I take the change and the receipt and move to the waiting area.

When I sit down with my food across from Pete, I tell him what happened and he laughs. I can't help laughing either. I was not slick about the situation at all. I don't feel so warm and my hands are dry again and my bladder doesn't feel so full.

"When are you going to settle down?" Pete asks. "You're after chicks all the time."

"Never, man. Never," I say. "Why should I? With so much PP everywhere?"

"Serious?" He eats the last bit of his burger.

"I don't know. Right now it's the farthest thing from my mind, man. I'm only 20. I've got years and years before I've even got to think about it. But then again, I don't have a mother on me going, *So when are you going to marry a nice Greek girl?*"

Pete is Greek. His parents are from Greece. They speak English pretty well. So do mine. They're from Brazil. They came here when I was barely two years old. But they learned, man, they learned. You've got to try and you've got to work hard, that's what they've always said. That's why I'm here at Triton Community College. Driving distance from home. With my best friend. I'm almost done with my second year and then I am outta here. I'm going to NIU in Dekalb and get my degree in Business. Gotta have a degree to get anywhere. And once at NIU I'll be doing everything possible to get into the panties of as many chicks as possible. Yeah-heah. I'm betting it's going to be much easier than here at this fuckin' lame ass community college. It's fine for what it is, but it sucks when it comes to gettin' laid. It's not like there's a "college community" at a community college. Not like at a real college like Northern Illinois. I know some people that went right away to NIU and they say there're chicks everywhere who are ready and willing all the time. Now that's the college for me.

He shakes his head and picks up some of his fries. "I swear, sometimes I want to smack her. It's like every day, now. Every day."

"You should get your own place, man. Then you won't have to listen to her anymore. Who wants to settle down, now?" I take another bite of my Whopper.

"That's what I keep telling her," he says.

"Get your own place."

"But then I've got to pay rent."

"Bummer, man. But freedom costs money." I grab some fries and dip them in some ketchup. Good stuff. My stomach is filling up. The place is filling up. The line by the registers is much longer than it was when I came in. I got here at a good time. And this table is ours until we decide to give it up.

"That's the truth."

"So then you've got to set your mother straight, but do it nice. You know, not be a jerk about it," I say. His mom is nice but real pushy. Mine's more laid back. She doesn't have my life planned out for me.

"Some way."

"You gotta be slick about it, man."

He nods. "I know, I know."

"You've got to slick it up. That's how you get through life, man. That's how you get through. Slicking it up. Whether it's your boss or a pussy. You gotta slick things up. It makes everything smooth, man."

"But you have to know how."

"That's true. But think of it like this: it's like Reagan. He was so smooth, he made all those TV reporters sound stupid. It didn't matter if he was right or wrong, he was so smooth it made him seem right all the time. Now *that* is the way to go. What we need is that special Reagan Teflon for attracting chicks. Can you see it? *Reagan Teflon Attraction now available for Men. Deflects accusations and attracts women.*"

"Reagan was very slick," he says.

"Exactly," I say.

"Bush is boring."

"But that's not fair to Bush. Pretty much everyone is boring next to Reagan."

"Definitely."

"So, now you know what you have to do." I take another big bite of my Whopper.

"Easy for you. You're going to be on your own next year," he says.

I stop chewing. I can taste all the mixed up flavors of cheese, meat, tomato, pickle, and lettuce. He closes his book. It's for his 19th century American History class. He's not going to be with me. That's a total bummer. He's my best friend. We've been through a lot. In high school we used to practice wrestling together during the off-season. We made each other better. Much better. That's the kind of friends we are. Always helping each other out. Of course, when we wrestled, we used to joke about who would be the farmer and who would be the sheep. I need to help him go to NIU with me. I chew fast, gulp it down, and take a quick sip of my coke.

I lean in. "You could be, too. There's still time, man. You could transfer. Just like I'm doing."

"I don't think I can do it."

"Sure you can," I say, taking another bite of my Whopper. A couple is standing in line, holding hands. Now he's got his arms around her from behind as they look up at the menu. She's hot. I wouldn't mind being in his position. I bet he's bangin' her every day.... It would be so cool to have a girlfriend to have sex with and hang out with like that all the time. Always with me. Not having to get her drunk to bring out the mood. Have it be a regular part of the relationship. Movies. Romantic stuff like driving into the city and walking along Oak Street beach at night.

"You think so?" He doesn't look all that confident. I don't know what it is with Pete. Sometimes, you have to talk him into thinking he can do something. He doesn't believe he can do certain things, like make the wrestling team or go to college.

"Sure. Just get an application and fill it out. How many credits do you have?"

"I'm not sure."

"Then find out. It's easy, man. It's not that hard. Then we can get an apartment together. And then no parents to tiptoe around. We can be banging chicks all the time."

"Sounds like a plan," he says.

"Dude, after lunch I'll show you where to get a transcript request form. And I'll show you how to request an application."

"Cool. Thanks, man."

"Hey, man, I know you'd do the same for me." I eat the last bit of my Whopper. I'm so glad Pete's my friend. The best guy I've ever known. We grew up together in Fairview, we're going to Triton together, and now we'll got to NIU together. Friends for life. We'll always be together, one way or another. I'm a lucky guy to have a friend like him. Pete finishes his drink. All that's left on his tray is the empty burger wrapper, the empty fries box, and his empty paper drink cup. I reach across the table and grab his textbook. *U.S. History: From the Louisiana Purchase to the Closing of the Frontier.* He's had a tough time with this class. He failed the first exam. Got C's on the second and third ones. I flip through the pages and lean back. He crumbles up the burger wrapper and tucks it into the empty fries box. I aced this class last semester. It was a breeze. Gettysburg. By the people for the people. Black and white pictures of dirty tired soldiers. Poor bastards. We're lucky. *The History of Martin and Pete: Volume I: High School. Volume II: Triton. Volume III—*

"I gotta go," he says.

I close the book. It used to be mine. At the end of last semester when he told me he was going to be taking the class I told him he could have my book. No sense in buying one since

I already had it.

"Come on," he says. "I'm gonna be late."

I hand it to him. He adds it to his pile of books. I grab the Coke and put the straw in my mouth. I sip a little bit. The plastic cover to the cup has those round buttons to show the kind of drink, three of 'em. I push each one in. I sip until there's nothing left except ice.

He stands up with his books and his tray.

"You workin' out later today?"

He shakes his head. "No. Not today. I got something else to do."

I've got to pee real bad now. All this caffeine. "Like what?"

"Nothing big. I'll call you later."

"What about the application and the transcripts? You still want to do that?"

"Dude, not today."

"Okay."

Pete walks away. If not today, then when? He passes the line to the registers. When? Tomorrow? This summer? He stops. Next semester, when I'm gone?... He might never do it.... He empties his tray into the garbage can by the far door and leaves. Through the tall windows I see him go back along the same sidewalk I took on my way here. Some people pass him. Farther and farther. Now I can't see him through all the people.

A third of my fries are left. But I'm not that hungry anymore and with my drink empty I've got nothing to wash the fries down with.

Volume 1, Wonderful!
An Iceman Review: Leon Katz's *Classical Monologues*
The Iceman

The Iceman has just finished Leon Katz's *Classical Monologues: From Aeschylus to Bernard Shaw, Volume 1, Younger Men's Roles.* It is wonderful! This is the first of a series, of which *Volume 1* and *Volume 2* (for younger and older men, respectively) are presently available and *Volume 3* and *Volume 4* (monologues for younger and older women) are due out in the fall of 2003. The Iceman has begun to probe the pages of *Volume 2, Older Men's Roles.* He has little doubt that it, too, will prove wonderful and he is of steadfast confidence that the succeeding volumes will be wonderful! Wonderful!, as well.

The Iceman spies a smiling single malt. The invitation is considered. He smiles instead upon the text before him. The four volumes exceed 500 monologues. Shakespeare is absent by design. The Bard is readily available and his omission allows for a more generous collection of other worthies, both celebrated and obscure, than would otherwise be possible. Roman drama is absent from *Volume 1* but Seneca is well represented in *Volume 2.* Eliot's citation for his poem "Marina," *"Quis hic locus, quae reio, quae mudni plaga,"* is there, from *Mad Hercules:* "What place is this? What realm?"

One would expect (and is not disappointed in) generous samplings of Marlowe, Cornielle, Racine. One is delighted to discover that the great speculative martyr of the Renaissance, Giordano Bruno, is represented by a foray into comedy. Who knew?

In the presence of the Inquisition, Bruno intoned: "You pronounce sentence upon me with greater fear than I who receive it."

Earlier, in the comic spirit of *Il Candelaio,* Bruno had asked a prospective lover to "...quench the passion that consumes me and which I cannot believe will lessen even with death."

Our knowledge of the Inquisition and the subsequent auto-da-fé renders the comedic pronouncement more telling than the merest of amusements. Later in *Volume 1* we contemplate Byron contemplating Manfred in anticipation of the romantic turbulence about to engulf his century:

> *And thou, the bright eye of the universe,*
> *That openest over all, and unto all*
> *Art a delight—thou shin'st not on my heart.*

These are some few favorites from dozens that could have just as easily been selected. Background information on the authors, plots, characters, and intentions preface each selection. Leon Katz is a great dramatist and dramaturge. These volumes attest to a stature acknowledged throughout the theatrical world. One wanders through these woods at the threat of civilization and an education surpassing several lifetimes. Professor Katz offers his selection from the purview of the celebrated one he presently entertains.

The Iceman commendeth each volume with clarity of mind that is rare in his reviewing experience—he finds, therefore (with scarcely a drop in sight), his glass full to overflowing.

Noose
Lisa Haviland

> *...Why should we hear about body bags and deaths and how many, what day it's going to happen, and how many this or what do you suppose? Oh, I mean, it's not relevant. So why should I waste my beautiful mind on something like that?...*

—Barbara Bush on ABC TV, March 20, 2003

The mind
an accessory
not beautiful
but brilliant
when worn by a woman.
But why bother?
balks our Babs.
Go for the slow kill,
the death of feminine
dissent, disarray
a pearl necklace
tied tight.

Otello: An Introduction to a Prayer
Essay by M.C. Gardner
Verdi's "Ave Maria" Performed by Susana Montal

In Harold Bloom's *Shakespeare, the Invention of the Human,* we find:

> *...the worship of Shakespeare ought to be even more a secular religion than it already is... After Jesus, Hamlet is the most cited figure in Western consciousness; no one prays to him, but no one evades him for long either.*

Verdi felt the same conviction for the protagonist of a different play. *Otello* is an opera of dark passion and spiritual sublimity. The librettist/composer, Boito, felt daunted by the scale of it. He took his libretto to the retired elder statesman of Italian opera. Only a masterpiece of the highest order could have tempted Verdi to once again scale the floorboards of La Scala. He knew that only the loftiest of themes and the greatest of his tragic scores would justify a return to the stage. The inclusion of an "Ave Maria," not found in Shakespeare, suggests that Verdi and Boito thought the tragedy, as well, a *Passion Play.*

There is strong evidence that Shakespeare's tragedy is a secular reenactment of events that unfolded fifteen centuries before he again took up the theme. Nietszche said that there was only one Christian—and that he died on the cross. One need not be Christian to be moved by the Christian myth or to use it as a subtext in one's art.

In the year of Shakespeare's birth, Michelangelo died while working on the marble of his final masterpiece—the Rondanini Pieta. With it he pared away the final months of his life and, as well, any hint of musculature and flesh on the bodies of Mary and the dead Christ. The Rondanini Pieta is a valediction to his art and life. He sculpted the quintessence of spirit from the intransigence of stone—and then he died.

By stressing the purity of Desdemona's spirit over the confused exigencies of Othello's flesh, Shakespeare, as well, sculpted an essence as pure as that which the sculptor had hewn from the stone. Desdemona is the most completely spiritual character that the poet would ever pen. She is a counterpart to Michelangelo's Pieta—but here Shakespeare accomplishes the double miracle of implying the divinely sensual Desdemona to be both the mother of God and the sacrificed son, lovingly cradled in her arms.

Shakespeare's "negative capability" (his ability to disappear within the consciousness of his characters) makes any inference as to his own beliefs a dubious enterprise. However, the sentiments of Shakespeare's clowns do, in the very least, offer ironic commentary on facets of his drama.

At the beginning of Act III we have such a clown.* It is not off-point to see that, at first, he speaks the merest burlesque. He disdains a musician's art as "wind instruments that speak to the nose." Yet, in a masterpiece of this magnitude we should be suspect of any passage found by the critics to be of "little consequence."

Othello has sent the clown to dismiss the musicians:

> CLOWN: *But, masters, here's money for you; and the general so likes your music that he desires you, for love's sake, to make no more noise with it.*
>
> MUSICIAN: *Well, sir, we will not.*
>
> CLOWN: *If you have any music that may not be heard, to't again. But, as they say, to hear the music, the general does not really care.*
>
> MUSICIAN: *We have none such, sir.*
>
> CLOWN: *Then put up your pipes... for I'll away. Go vanish into air, away!*

---

* I am indebted to Professor Harold C. Goddard for directing my thoughts to the deserving, though much neglected, clown of the third act. We differ in the direction the unheard music leads us, but his reading of Shakespeare remains one of the most humane and provocative of the last century.

If we follow the hint of a "music that may *not* be heard," we need look no further to the harmony Othello is thwarted from enjoying—the music of Desdemona. Shakespeare takes pains to keep the action at a frenzied, unconsummated sexual pitch. This ratchets up the tension, but also brings to mind the unconsummated union of Mary and Joseph, as related in the Gospels.

Other hints are scattered throughout the text. The first (and not the least telling) is the first word that Iago utters: "'Sblood." For Iago it is simply an expletive tossed off to Roderigo, but in the Elizabethan lexicon 'sblood is a contraction of "God's blood."

Where might the trail of *God's blood* lead us in a drama about the murder of innocence? Most readers of the play believe Desdemona to be killed by suffocation—either strangulation or beneath a pillow. But within a line of the stage direction: "He smothers her," we have Othello asking three questions.

> *What noise is this? Not dead? Not quite dead?*

And,

> *I that am cruel am yet merciful. I would not have*
> *thee linger in thy pain. So, so.*

How he attempts to end her pain in the interval of that "So, so" is the point of conjecture. Goddard believes he stabs her with the same instrument with which he ends his own life. For purposes of these reflections I ask the reader to remember another soldier, a Centurion who pierced the side of a fabled innocent nailed upon a plank before him. For if Christ takes the sins of the world upon himself in Gethsemane, so, as well, does Desdemona, upon her deathbed.

In answer to Emilia's impassioned query,

> *Who hath done this deed?*

Desdemona responds,

> *Nobody—I myself.*

And as Christ concludes his agony with:

> *Lord, into thy hands I commend my spirit,*

so also, Desdemona concludes her own with,

> *Commend me to my kind lord. O, farewell.*

The stage direction "[She dies.]" follows immediately. God's blood, indeed.

Othello's own judgment of her murder is usually read from the Quarto,

> *One whose hand, like the base Indian, threw a*
> *pearl away richer than his tribe.*

But the folio reading is,

> *One whose hand, like the base Judean, threw a*
> *pearl away richer than his tribe.*

This allusion to Judas, taken with "I kissed thee ere I killed thee," is as exact a parallel to a subtext as any found in Shakespeare. The play is, of course, larger than any schemata attempting to elucidate its mysteries. But Shakespeare, more than any major writer, was drawn to the mystery of consciousness and so became a master of it. He knew that there was nothing good nor bad but thinking makes it so—yet Macbeth sups full of horrors. Ghosts, witches, and portents are restive in the wings and at any moment the wild mares of night might trample forth from gaping fissures found in earth or mind. Hamlet ponders the undiscovered country from whose bourne no traveler returns. Falstaff babbles of green fields as death climbs from foot to knee to thigh, and the doctor in Macbeth remarks that Lady Macbeth's inability to wash the blood from her hands needs "more the divine than the physician." These beliefs belong to their characters; they are the manifest of their consciousness.

Of what consciousness did Shakespeare imbue Desdemona? Othello says of her, after relating tales of his adventures:

> *She wished heaven had made her such a man.*

It is only when we remember that Shakespeare delights in

commingling the sexes (of his more highly evolved characters) that the second meaning of her wish emerges.

She wished heaven had made her such a man.

This under-meaning is thrown in greater relief by Othello's exclamation, greeting her upon arrival from the storm:

O my fair warrior!

Each speaks to an otherworldly strength, as much beyond gender as Christ was believed to be beyond mortality. The correspondence between the one tale and the other is purely allusive, but its cumulative effect grows with each reading. It might seem a stretch to suggest that Desdemona's "Nobody, I myself" is shorthand for Christ's atonement.

We are prepared for this alignment at an earlier juncture in the text. In Act 4, Scene 1, Desdemona speaks of her desire to reconcile Othello with Cassio:

I would do much t'atone them.

Overhearing this, Othello rages atonement's exact opposite:

Fire and brimstone!

He calls her a devil and then strikes her to the floor and repeats the charge:

O Devil, Devil!

Act 4, Scene 2 is one of the most psychologically devastating in the world's literature. In it, as he does in the 3rd act of the opera, Othello considers his wife's claim of innocence:

Is it possible?

Desdemona grasps at the hope his seeming doubt has proclaimed. She exclaims,

O heaven, forgive us!

She melts before the prospect of their reconciliation. In his,

> *I cry you, mercy then.*

Desdemona believes that heaven has granted light to their love's renewal. But it is a feint and a false hope. The complete line reads:

> *I cry you mercy then, I took you for the cunning*
> *whore of Venice, that married with Othello.*

He then tosses coins in her face as payment for the pleasures he imagines she shared with Cassio. In the episode that follows Shakespeare explores another of his psychological reversals. Desdemona unknowingly summons the one person responsible for her misfortunes. At the nadir of her consciousness she confronts Shakespeare's greatest villain at the absolute height of his own—she summons Iago. The ever-voluble Iago is, here, near speechless in the face of her beauty and pain. Far from *being* a whore, she can not even speak the word. She asks Iago: "Am I that name?"

The "good" incapable of utterance and "evil" rendered mute by the purity of its flame. It is a prelude of his final silence. The defeat of the Turbaned Turk begins here. In the face of this "fair warrior" he can barely link words together in a phrase: "What is the matter, lady?" and "What name, fair lady?' His "Do not weep, do not weep," suggests something of her effect upon him. She calls him "good friend" and kneels before him as Christ had knelt before Pilate.

And when Emilia proclaims that some cozening slave, to get office, has devised the slanders under which she suffers, Desdemona replies: "If any such there be, heaven pardon him." Only on Calgary do we find anything of its equal. And only in a desert temptation do we find the equal of Desdemona's

> *Beshrew me if I should do such a wrong for the*
> *whole world.*

That is her strength and the world's hope. The Roman Empire learned that of Christ. The British Empire learned it of Gandhi. The reader learns it again, of Desdemona at the end of Act 4 as she concludes:

> *Good night, good night. Heaven me, such uses*
> *send, not to pick bad from bad but by bad mend.*

In Act 5, Othello pronounces Desdemona to be on her deathbed; her "banish me, my lord, but kill me not," echoes the "Father, let this cup pass from my lips" of the Gospels. Othello confirms her fate: "Thou art to die." Desdemona replies: "Then Lord have mercy on me." And Othello concludes: "I say amen." In those three words Othello has usurped heaven and found himself at the center of Dante's frozen hell. The "I say amen" is also the Christian God confirming that the cup shall not pass from the lips of the anointed one. Othello tells Desdemona that her death is not a murder, but a sacrifice.

Near the end of Act 4, Scene 3, Desdemona speaks again of atonement. If we remember that atonement means *"at one-ment,"* that through God's grace, mental separateness, which is the prerogative of passion and sin, is resolved in the *"at one-ment"* of divine union, we shouldn't be surprised to hear Desdemona declare, in the final hour of her life:

> *All's one. Good Father how foolish are our minds.*

And then to Emilia,

> *If I do die before, prithee, shroud me in these same*
> *sheets.*

Here Shakespeare and Verdi follow with the pathos and resignation of the "Willow Song." Following it, Verdi provides the prayer that Othello only inquires about in the play: "Hath thou prayed tonight?" Desdemona's, "Ay, my Lord" precedes her murder.

In the opera, however, Verdi desires that we *hear* the music that "may not be heard," requested by the clown in Act 3. Mayhaps, had Othello *heard* Desdemona's transcendental prayer, his "I say amen," might have been the benediction to a far different play. Here now is Susana Montal's interpretation of the "Ave Maria" aria from Verdi's *Otello*.

Download Susana Montal's performance of Verdi's "Ave Maria" at www.anotheramerica.org/avemaria.

The Contributors

Shelley Berman

...is one of the world's abiding performers and writers, and a senior professor at the University of Southern California Department of Professional Writing.

Scott Chamberlin

...is a freelance writer, editor, and designer living in Venice, California.

Tyler Craft Cormney

...is a master's candidate in the USC Graduate Professional Writing Program.

Lance Fogan

...is a retired Kaiser Permanente neurologist, 1971-97. Currently he is a UCLA School of Medicine Professor of Neurology, teaching part-time. He remains a full-time family man. His special hobby is "Shakespeare and his medical knowledge."

Donald Freed

...is a prize-winning author and historian.

Patricia Rae Freed

...lives with her husband, Donald, and her dog, Emma, in their Westwood home.

M.C. Gardner

...is a playwright, essayist, and editor.

Mary Gilvarry

…was born in Harlem three quarters of a century ago. The Irish Catholic enclave, in which she was raised, is her primary subject.

Lisa Haviland

…is a graduate student at USC and a poet.

Richard Hellinga

…born and raised in the Chicago area and a graduate of the Graduate Professional Writing Program at USC, is a writer living in Los Angeles.

Nina Hiken

…has been living and writing in Los Angeles for 14 years. The included excerpt is from her novel in progress, *Becoming Ms. Hiken.*

The Iceman

…ran guns for the Republican expeditionary force during the invasion of Majorca. He is mentioned with affection in the memoirs of Captain Manuel Uribarri.

Leon Katz

…is currently a professor of theater at UCLA and professor emeritus of drama at Yale University.

Charles Kruger

…currently works as a middle- and high-school teacher in South Central Los Angeles, and is a member of the Los Angeles Poets and Writers Collective.

Francine Kubrin

…was born in 1932 in Los Angeles, where she has lived continuously. She graduated from California State University, Northridge, in 1974 with honors in English. She has worked as a hospital librarian for twenty-six years.

A.J. Langguth

... is a professor at USC and the author, most recently, of *Our Vietnam*.

Frances Luban

...is an art historian and psychotherapist. Her documentary, "Joyce Treiman: the Artist as Voyeur," has been shown on PBS. "A Quiet Life" is part of a novel she is writing.

Ara Mgrdichian

...is a teacher and a writer.

Kristine Hren Moe

...is a graduate of USC's Graduate Professional Writing Program. The short story "Orange Diamonds," which inspired the current novel in progress, appeared in *PMS poem/memoir/story*, a writers' quarterly from the University of Alabama at Birmingham, and was a finalist in the So to Speak Short-Short Fiction Contest in 2001.

Susana Montal

...is a writer, composer, and musician.

Adrienne Nater

...is a teacher and writer. She is also an aviator of note and a champion surfer.

Harold Pinter

... is a great dramatist, poet, and human rights exponent.

Barbara Ponse

...is a psychotherapist in private practice and a writer living in Malibu. She holds a doctorate in Sociology from USC and taught at Washington University in St. Louis. She is the author of a monograph and several articles about the social construction of identity, secrecy, and stigma. "My Mother and the Virgin Mary" is a selection from a forthcoming collection of short stories.

Portia Putnam

...is a college administrator, professor, poet, and playwright.

James Ragan

...is an internationally recognized poet and playwright and the Director of the USC Graduate Professional Writing Program. Translated into 12 languages, he has performed for five heads of state including Presidents Gorbachev and Havel. Ragan has been praised by Nobel Prize nominee Miroslav Holub as "a poet who dominates the art of image, the art of poetic line, with an insight that marks major poets."

Stephanie Silberstein

...teaches freshman writing at USC. "Blind Date" is her first published story.

Kevin "Bumdog" Torres

...is a poet, street singer, and playwright, currently without a forwarding address.

William Wasz

...was born and reared in Manassas, Virginia in the mid-1950s. In 1994, he was arrested while driving actress/model Paula Barbieri's vehicle, which was later determined to contain serious evidence in the O.J. Simpson trial. However, Mr. Wasz was to go down in the annals of government cover-up. At the age of 39, he is seeking redemption through participation in social programs and his literary work; such notables as Noam Chomsky, Donald Freed, Jerry Stahl, and Dan Bessie have supported his voice and work.